Praise for *I Am Enough*:

"*I Am Enough* chronicles the personal odyssey of Danielle Saputo from quiet compliant girl to strong confident woman, heir, coach, advisor and ultimately, inspiration. It is a deeply remarkable memoir that carries the reader along, provoking a multitude of thoughts and feelings along the way. You will be entranced by her journey and its compelling destination, a place of peace called Resilience."

> — James Grubman, PhD
> Family wealth consultant and author of *Strangers in Paradise: How Families Adapt to Wealth Across Generations*

"It is rare when we get true insight into another's life journey—especially from those whom we place on a pedestal in our society. Danielle, through warmth, vulnerability and wit, shares her transformation from *Never Being Enough* to *Living in the Light*. Her absorbing prose inspires us to have courage to challenge our own disempowering stories, build a 'sage mindset' and liberate ourselves to be true and authentic by embracing all that we are. Nestled in this book is a gift—an opportunity for each of us to more deeply reflect on our own journey and design who we want to be as we move forward. It is an endearing story and a must read!"

> — Wendy Sage-Hayward, MA, FEA
> The Family Business Consulting Group, Helping
> Family Businesses Prosper Across Generations

"Saputo's brave, raw and authentic message in *I Am Enough* offers readers a path for understanding what wealth is and is not. For anyone growing up in the shadow and confusion of abundance, prepare to unlearn everything you thought you knew about preparing yourself and your heirs."

— Tom Deans, PhD
Author of *Every Family's Business and Willing Wisdom*

"This intimate and delightfully voiced book of small vignettes shares the author's story of self-discovery as she navigates life in the complex environment of one of Canada's most prominent business families. The universal lessons and very practical tools are shared with a deft touch that both belies the meatiness of the book and makes it accessible and relevant to everyone."

— Dr. Julie A. Morton, FEA, Q.Med
Chief Continuity Officer, Our Family Office, Inc.

"This is a must-read for any beneficiary finding themselves in this complicated world. I give Danielle major credit for being so honest, authentic, and transparent on her personal experience . . . so much inspiration and power in her prose!"

— Kirby Rosplock, PhD
Founder and CEO , Tamarind Partners

"Danielle shares her story of growth and evolution in a large Canadian business family. Her honest account reveals her triumphs and challenges as she victoriously learns to find her own voice, purpose, and flame. Throughout the book, Danielle passes on her lessons learned and provides valuable guidance for those growing up in the shadows of hugely successful families."

— Richard Voss,
Certified Financial Planner

I Am Enough

Emerging from the Shadows into the Sunlight of My True Self

Danielle Saputo

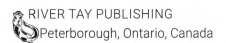
RIVER TAY PUBLISHING
Peterborough, Ontario, Canada

I Am Enough:
Emerging from the Shadows into the Sunlight of My True Self
© 2022, Danielle Saputo. All rights reserved.
Published by River Tay Publishing, Peterborough, Ontario, Canada

ISBN 978-1-7782127-2-7 (Hardcover)
ISBN 978-1-7782127-0-3 (Paperback)
ISBN 978-1-7782127-1-0 (eBook)

www.DanielleSaputo.com

All photographs are from the author's collection. "I Am Enough—A Poem about Worthiness" © 2019 Jennifer Williamson. Used with permission.

This book is intended to provide accurate information with regard to its subject matter and reflects the opinion and perspective of the author. However, in times of rapid change, ensuring all information provided is entirely accurate and up-to-date at all times is not always possible. Therefore, the author and publisher accept no responsibility for inaccuracies or omissions and specifically disclaim any liability, loss or risk, personal, professional or otherwise, which may be incurred as a consequence, directly or indirectly, of the use and/or application of any of the contents of this book.

To my parents:

Franco and Lia Saputo, who have given me a strong
foundation upon which to thrive. I am forever grateful.

To my husband:

Corrado, the door is open for me to step through,
experience and grow. Thank you for this freedom.

To my girls:

Enrica, Olivia, Aurelia, you are the reason I want to bring
my best self forward. I love you with all my heart.

I wrote every word of this book with you in mind, my darling
girls, to drive home the point that owning your history, using
your voice, living mindfully in the present and grabbing hold
of your future potential with both hands is your birthright.
The choice to live in a state of positivity is yours, yours
alone. You don't have to wait for anyone's permission to
realize that you have that power. I'm telling you now, while
you're still young, that as you grow older you must let your
light shine as brightly as the sun so you will bloom and
prosper on your own terms and no one else's, not even mine.

I Am Enough—A Poem about Worthiness

There is a wholeness that's already mine.
It's already ours.
I am not just the seed,
I am the rain that waters the flower.
It's a reality that's already there,
That I am enough.
I take on faith
That wholeness is already mine,
That I need do nothing to deserve,
That my worthiness is based only on my being.

I am wise enough to let go,
And I am strong enough to remember the truth
Of who I really am.
I can encounter the world
In such a way
That I remember who I am.

I am the rest inside the unrest.
I am the depth of the sky,
And the light piercing the sea.
I am the crest of a wave.
All that I need to be,
I am.

There is no problem to solve in this moment.
There is no plan to make,
No failure to be feared,
No other place to be.

This moment is enough.
This place is enough.
This imperfection is enough.
I am patient enough for my life to unfold in divine timing.

I feel the fullness of my life in this moment.
I feel the richness of my life in this space.
I am loved beyond thought,
And I have nothing to prove.
There is no one to impress.
I receive the message
That being is enough.

I am wise enough to see magic through a child's eyes.
I am resilient enough to see past the pain.
I am kind enough to realize
That my worth has been with me
This whole time.

Beyond the shadows
That I have created,
The message remains:
I am the same.
I have always been enough,
Simply by being here.
Simply by being.

It only takes a moment,
And I remember this again.

— Jennifer Williamson[1]

Contents

Prologue

OVERVIEW

You are enough just as you are.
— Munna

This is the story of a girl who grew up in the shadow of her large family tree. While her family gave her many comforts in her life, she fell into the shadow of this tree and silenced herself from sharing her accomplishments, eclipsed by the success and perceived expectations of others. She had an inner voice telling her that she was never good enough.

As she grew up, she reflected on many life-defining moments and learned how to overcome that voice in her head and, as a result, how to balance the paradox of being her true self while still finding her place in her loving, wealthy and supportive family. Only then did her essence shine through the branches of the tree and bring sunlight to her life, which she now shares with others.

As she continued to show up for herself every day as her best self, she came to understand that she is enough.

THE JOURNEY

Life is a matter of choices and every
choice you make makes you.
— John C. Maxwell

E merging from my family's shadow and stepping into the light has been a journey fifty years in the making. The success I've experienced along the way has been in the journey itself and not in arriving at any particular destination. In other words, the journey itself was what mattered. Any success I've had was a result of the journey. And the journey continues. As I've travelled this occasionally rocky path over the last half century, I've learned many lessons about how to discern what's true in my life and what's merely perceived, what's important and what's trivial, and the power of living with intention. It has been an eye-opening voyage. Unfortunately, there is no cut-and-dried road map for taking a trip such as this. Who am I to say that what has worked for me will work for you? The best I can do is open my heart and share my personal story of discovery with you here, in the hope that it will resonate and perhaps even inspire you in your own expedition of self-discovery. In the pages that follow, I will share:

- What it was like growing up in one of Canada's most prominent entrepreneurial families, including some of the positive lessons from my elders and siblings as well as the defining moments that tested me and caused me to retreat into the shadows.

- The negative stories, limiting self-beliefs and lack of accountability that blocked me from developing myself to my full potential and the approach I used to overcome them. I'll also share stories from my coaching clients[2] and the steps we took—steps you, too, can take—to move forward with confidence.

- My "Bottom-Line Questions" for regaining equilibrium when the going gets tough and other tips for setting a positive, winning mindset for growth.

- Why and how to find an accountability partner to help you conquer every saboteur who tries to derail you on your journey back to your authentic self.

- How your mindset, whether fixed in place or open to growth, impacts your decision-making process.

- Lots of valuable parenting tips designed to help build your children's confidence and healthy sense of self.

- My counterintuitive method for establishing yourself as a legacy leader in any situation, including in your interactions with your family members, so every person shares their potential.

- How you can "party your way to personal growth." I'll share a few ideas for celebrating your progress and maintaining your momentum.

- A list of recommended books and videos that will bring more positivity and focus into your life.

If you were born into the younger generations of an affluent family and you're sitting in the shadow when it comes to your identity, personal fulfillment and sense of self-worth, this book is for you. If you are the patriarch or matriarch of a successful entrepreneurial dynasty and you want to understand what life is like for your children and grandchildren, this book is also for you. If you're a parent and not from an affluent family, there is insight for you here as well.

We are tasked with defining ourselves in this lifetime. As one who was born with a well-known last name, I know this is easier said than done. It can be done; it *must* be done. If I can do it, so can you. My mission with this book (and with my coaching and family advising work) is to shine the light on your greatness until you can no longer ignore it. Your greatness is in there, trust me. No patriarch/matriarch handed it to you on a silver platter, and no one—no matter how commanding or accomplished or charismatic they may be—has the power to take it away from you unless you decide to give it to them. It belongs to you and you alone.

It takes a personal journey to discover the authentic essence of who you are. Let's go find it together. Let's bring it out into the sunshine and allow it to run free, as it was intended to do. What you do and how you choose to react is your choice. The choice is yours. The choice to live in a state of positivity is yours and yours alone.

THE MASKS WE WEAR

You cannot teach a man anything;
you can only help him discover it within himself.
— Galileo

"No. Not now," my father said.

His tone and the way he used his words brought a clear message: Stop. Yet I pointed out once again that our family's legacy was in peril unless we talked about how we would transfer our wealth from one generation to the next. My father suddenly pounded his hand on the table.

"Danielle, are you not grateful for *anything*?"

My heart felt as though it had been ripped from my chest. I looked to my mother and siblings for support as they sat in stunned silence. I left the table, closed myself in the washroom and cried as I've never cried before. I could not stop the uncontrollable sobs that washed over me, and I didn't want to stop. I allowed the tears to flow and my body to shake. As much as that exchange broke my heart and shattered my confidence, it ultimately led to me looking at why my family interacted the way it did and why I responded the way I did. Since then, I have learned how to help others be more resilient, in life and in business.

First, I had to face the mask I'd been wearing my entire life—that saboteur's voice that always nagged in the background. It obscured my view in ways that I had never considered before. Only then could I see the light beyond the shadow of my family tree.

After that traumatic family meeting, which took place in March of 2016, I turned to the company of people like me: people in their twenties and thirties, born into ultra-affluent families, who wished to develop their leadership potential. Although I was a little older than the other participants in this Next Generation Leadership Program (I was well into my forties), I was invited to attend for what I believed was a key reason. I believed that my input as a third-generation business family member—caught in the sandwich generation of caring for parents and children simultaneously—would be of value.

As I embarked upon this journey, I knew only one thing for certain: I was unfulfilled at that moment and I didn't know how to fix it. I had all the elements in my life that could have allowed me to run smoothly on a full tank—a tank filled with love, joy and abundance—yet I lurched around feeling empty inside.

The Next Gen Leadership Program, which took place over five days in May of 2016, was titled the Scone Project. It took place in Scone Palace, a lovely historic castle in Scotland. Here, I had my first meaningful glimpse into what was troubling me. An important part of the Scone Project was to identify the false stories we told ourselves, because our behaviour was usually based on these distorted truths. Once we identified what was not true, our behaviour and outlook could change for the better. As the facilitator explained it, these stories are like masks that we hide behind, and it was time to identify our false stories.

The concept was outlined as follows:

> We all have a story, a story that has molded us, influenced us, and sometimes the story has become us. Where does such a story, one that can have *so much* influence over us, come from? Where is it born? How does it grow? Here is where one's story comes from and is born: An event occurs in our life, and as a result of that event we make up a story about the event. Another way to say this is we attach a subjective meaning to the event. We all wear the masks to compensate and hide our story from the world to see. Yet what we desperately want and desire is to be accepted and be loved for who we are. There is an irony here, which it may take a while to see: When one shows themselves fully without the mask, when one shows the world their real self, story and all, then one may get what they are so desperately seeking—to be loved and accepted. What is the story you are trying to cover up with the mask you wear? What is your mask?

Each of us was given a white face mask, the kind you get at a dollar store that covers the top half of your face, with eyeholes and a thin elastic band that slips over your head to hold it in place. We were also provided with paint, stickers, feathers, sequins—all kinds of interesting embellishments we could use to decorate our creations.

Working on my mask was similar to watching an old Polaroid photograph develop. With each embellishment I applied, the picture of my limiting belief came into sharper focus until at last, I held in my hands the mask that said it all. Although it was cheerful and bright and covered with sparkly stars and feathers, I had written in bold letters across the front these three damning words:

NEVER GOOD ENOUGH

My tears fell like rain as I realized in that moment that this was the story I had told myself since I was a child. It came in many different phrases, but the meaning was the same:

My voice does not matter.

I don't make a difference.

No one hears me.

I am insignificant.

I am just a number.

I am never good enough.

Looking back, it's no mystery why I felt this way. Even something as harmless as the family supper table fed into my feelings of inadequacy. For my family of seven—my parents, four sisters and me—suppertime was about sharing a meal and the news of our day. As we ate, my sisters, three older and one younger than me, would speak with great enthusiasm about what they'd done at school or in their various other activities. As each girl took her moment to shine, I would sit silently, politely listening to what they were saying yet not participating. I finally realized that I didn't participate because nobody asked me to. In my mind, there was only one reason that they hadn't turned to me for news, advice or feedback: I and my thoughts were irrelevant.

The one time I recall talking about my day at the dinner table, I announced that I had received a 96 percent mark on a math test, only to be asked, "Why didn't you get one hundred?" This was just the right "food" to feed my insecurity that I was "never good enough."

And add to that, this was no average family. We were the Saputo family, a name synonymous with the brand of a huge Canadian dairy enterprise. My identity was closely tied to—and overshadowed by—the pioneers who had built and maintained the business for two generations. Being a member of an ultra-affluent and prominent family, while undoubtedly having its advantages, can also be an emotional minefield, especially amongst the more sensitive like me.

Creating that mask began an emotional journey that has required total honesty about how others have treated me and also how I have treated myself. It was time to face my fears and reveal the real Danielle. Danielle with a capital *D* and not danielle with a little *d* as I was presenting myself every day at that time, shying away and not letting my own light shine through.

The challenging process of removing that mask eventually opened my eyes and my mind to unbelievable joys and possibilities. Before I could fully embrace my value and my life, I had to step back and look at how that mask had become an ingrained part of my identity in the first place.

This book unfolds in three parts:

1. My foundation—where I share stories about my elders and defining moments that fueled the limiting beliefs I had of myself. These defining moments come with great gratitude. Having a growth mindset has allowed me to forgive and move forward and continually grow, even though some moments were heartbreaking at the time. This is a reflection on my life's journey.

2. Creating my own legacy—where I branch out from the family, journey into parenthood and realize my limiting beliefs. At times I felt I had a superpower to do it all, and at the same time I felt so shadowed by the loved ones around me. This stage of my life taught me the paradox that it's not me or the family, it's both-and. When I'm strong, then the family is strong and it is not either-or. I share with the reader some parenting tips and tools I came across on my journey to my true self.

3. Lessons about myself—where I reflect back to my pivotal moment and the program that began my journey to my true self. I also share with my reader the wisdom I came across. I conclude with describing how I am enough and I find fulfillment by living my legacy.

In sharing the tools I came across on my journey to self-discovery, my goal is not to appear as a self-help expert. My intention is to share the tools that brought me one step closer to rediscovering my true self. As a life learner, I believe there is always another tool to share, and bringing together what has worked for me has made me my own guru on this journey of life. I'm sharing this journey with you.

Part 1—My Foundation

LIVING UP TO THE FAMILY NAME

All truths are easy to understand once uncovered.

—Galileo

Living up to the Saputo name was much easier said than done. My large, exuberant, affluent Italian family cast an exceptionally long, wide shadow. I buried myself deep within its shadow for many years without even knowing it, not realizing my full potential or claiming my rightful place at the table, whether it was in the kitchen of my childhood home or at a business meeting in my later years. Eventually, I learned that I was not alone in my feelings of insignificance, irrelevance and inadequacy, for this painful dilemma was fairly common amongst members of the second and third generations of prominent families like mine. From the outside it looks as if we have it made, yet inside we're prisoners of our own thoughts and feelings. It's extremely difficult to measure up to the patriarch and matriarch—the Empire Builders, the Creators of All That Is.

Many of us feel so daunted by the task that we don't even try, let alone even know why we are suffering. Or, as in my case, I tried so hard that I sacrificed myself in the process.

Parental Criticism and a Matter of Perception

> *Don't let compliments get to your head and*
> *don't let criticism get to your heart.*
>
> *— Lysa TerKeurst*

In her research, psychology professor and resilience researcher Dr. Suniya Luthar has discovered that excessive emphasis on an affluent child's accomplishments while growing up pressures us into feeling as though we cannot fail. Since children of affluence have ready access to so many opportunities to get a head start—such as private tutors, seminars, workshops and lessons galore—we have no excuse for real or *imagined* "failure" at anything we set out to do. As Dr. Luthar so simply puts it, "These youths come to believe there is one path to ultimate happiness—having money .... They grow preoccupied with becoming highly marketable commodities, pursuing activities chiefly if they will look good on résumés. There is scant time for exploration of who they are as individuals or for nurturing unique interests."[3]

Without this self-awareness, when a child of affluence faces parental criticism, or even the mere perception of it, they experience elevated levels of depression and anxiety. Dr. Luthar says that these individuals feel the pressure of "I can, therefore, I *must*."[4] The feeling that I had to be perfect in order to be worthy of my parents' acceptance was my personal affliction. My self-worth was entirely dependent on what my parents thought of me or, more likely, what I thought they thought of me. Parental disapproval doesn't have to be voiced to have a negative effect on my self-worth. It only has to be perceived. I perceived quite a bit of disapproval over the years.

Truth be told, I didn't need to read a bunch of studies to know that there are serious problems afflicting the younger generations of prominent families. Attend any private school function or any philanthropic event and you'll be surrounded by second- and third-generation people of affluence who are grappling with understanding their place in the world. They are struggling to define who they are and frantically seeking fulfillment, all the while suffering from intense guilt because they can't imagine why they feel so empty when they've been given so much.

Like so many of these people, I did not see my full value as a person.

> *Our deepest fear is not that we are inadequate. Our deepest fear is that we are powerful beyond measure. It is our light, not our darkness that most frightens us. We ask ourselves, Who am I to be brilliant, gorgeous, talented, fabulous? Actually, who are you not to be? Your playing small does not serve the world. We are all meant to shine. And as we let our own light shine, we unconsciously give other people permission to do the same. As we're liberated from our own fear, our presence automatically liberates others.*
> — *Marianne Williamson,* A Return to Love[5]

For a while, I did not see my full value as a person. I felt insignificant, questioning who I was and why I was there. Or, as author Marianne Williamson so eloquently puts it, I was playing small and not allowing my natural brilliance to shine through. By the time I was in my midforties, I desperately wanted to help myself out of this sad slump. Most of all, I wanted to do whatever I could to ensure that my three young daughters didn't suffer the same fate. With those lofty goals as my inspiration, I set out on a journey of self-discovery, which I've documented in this book. The stories I will relate here are according to my own recollection. Others may remember the events differently, and that's okay. We all have our own way of viewing the world.

THE FAMILY, THE BUSINESS AND THE HEROES WHO BUILT THEM

Families are like branches on a tree.
We grow in different directions, yet our roots remain as one.
— Unknown

My extended family's company, Saputo Inc., has been in operation in Montreal since 1954. My grandfather, Giuseppe Saputo, his wife and children (one of whom is my father, Franco) immigrated from Sicily to Montreal, with Giuseppe and my father being the first to arrive in November 1950. From humble beginnings and a difficult start on Canadian soil, Giuseppe and his family founded a small cheese manufacturing company that would eventually become the multinational dairy products powerhouse it is today. This was thanks in large part to my dad, who experimented with making cheese from the cow's milk at the farm where he worked upon arriving in Canada. By the time I was born in 1969, Saputo Inc. was in the midst of major expansion and "Saputo" was well on its way to becoming a household name throughout Canada. Today, the company's sixty manufacturing plants and fifteen thousand employees process annually more than ten billion litres of milk into dairy products that are offered for sale in forty countries around the world. In 2020, Saputo Inc. earned almost $15 billion in revenue, making the Saputo family one of the wealthiest in Canada.

Growing up, my four sisters and I were surrounded by the abundance our entrepreneurial elders had provided, although never to the point of opulence. I was given just enough material effects to feel secure, yet not enough to feel entitled by seeking any special treatment. Any money I had under my name was well earned and hard to come by. Still, my famous last name and my family's wealth and prominence created conflicts within me that troubled me for some time. I was so filled with gratitude for my parents' hard work and sacrifices that I allowed my own development to take a back seat as I focused on proving my love and appreciation for them. After all, I suspected that no matter what I managed to achieve in my life, I would never be able to build something as grand as they had. I made many assumptions about their expectations for me, assumptions that I let stunt my personal growth and stifle my voice.

The business my grandfather started was very much a part of the family when I was growing up. I spent many happy childhood hours lying on the floor outside my dad's presidential office in the factory in Saint-Michel, a neighbourhood in Montreal, peering through a window that looked down onto the manufacturing floor. From there, I watched the big stirring arms on the stainless-steel vats go back and forth to make the cheese. If I close my eyes and sit quietly for a moment, I can still hear the hum of the machines, smell that distinct aroma of cheese in the making and see the workers tending to the cheese-making process. The company was deeply rooted in my identity. For many years, in December I would deliver boxes of Saputo products to friends and teachers. When I was fifteen, I began working in the filing room at the factory and spent my summer breaks as a Saputo employee. I became a full-time employee in my midtwenties and continued working there until I married at thirty. That is a whole story in itself. To understand the full journey, I need to return to the formative years before then.

When I was a little girl living in Dollard-des-Ormeaux, a suburb of Montreal, my primary school was so close to our house that I could walk home for lunch every day. Once I arrived, my mother, Lia, would treat me to one of her legendary meals and a loving smile. She would always be there with her warm hands to welcome me and serve me a delicious meal. The Flintstones would be playing in the background, making the environment feel exactly right for a hungry little girl who loved cartoons. There is so much about my mom's cooking that is memorable. She's taken lots of traditional dishes and added her loving touch to them. My favourites are spedini (thin veal cutlets shaped into rolls filled with breadcrumbs, pine nuts, onion, cheese and more), manicotti (thin pasta sheets rolled and filled with ricotta and topped with a perfect tomato sauce), and the incredible way she prepares a shoulder blade roast. She makes a great chicken bake and incredible vegetable dishes too. She is truly a champion in the kitchen. If I had to choose only one thing to associate with my mother, it would be her presence in the kitchen, providing nourishment for us. Warm bellies, warm hearts—that was what she gave us.

When I was seven, we moved to Laval-sur-le-Lac and I started riding a big yellow school bus to and from my new school, ending my beloved lunchtime ritual. My sisters and I continued to spend many hours together as my mom ferried us to our activities. She would pick us up after school and take us straight to another activity that kept us growing and learning. When I became a mother, her message to me was, "Keep your children occupied with what they love to do and you will keep them out of trouble." That was her way. She was a nurturing parent.

Growing up, my mom was a homemaker extraordinaire. Even if she was exhausted, hurt or bothered, she presented a strong face. I don't believe I ever saw my mother sleep when I was a little girl. If she wasn't cooking or cleaning the house, she was downstairs at her treasured sewing machine. My mom spent countless late nights making us clothes, Halloween costumes, household items and décor. She was a master seamstress. When my sisters married, she made their bridesmaids' dresses, and when her grandchildren came along, she made darling clothing for them, including sweet little capes and coats. She also made every holiday season magical. As Christmas approached, we would go to bed one night with the house looking normal and wake up the next morning to find a fully decorated Yuletide wonderland. There would be a sparkling Christmas tree and snowmen and Santas everywhere. I would often wonder, When did all this get done? My mom would do the same thing for Thanksgiving, Halloween, Easter and every other occasion we were celebrating. There was always something in the house that brought forth the spirit of the holidays.

While my mother was a constant presence in our lives, I hardly ever saw my father, Franco. He worked at the cheese factory all the time. He would be gone before I woke up in the morning and wouldn't return home until after I was in bed at night. On the occasions when he was with us physically, he wasn't always with us mentally since his head was filled to overflowing with the challenges of running a rapidly expanding company. I didn't feel bad about his absence, and I don't recall ever holding it against him. It was the way it was.

Like many hardworking men of his era, my dad spent many Friday and Saturday nights playing cards with his family members and friends. These spirited card games usually took place in the basement at my aunt's house, where we would often go on weekends. We kids knew to never interrupt the adults, especially during a game of cards. Whenever we did venture into the basement we were as quiet as mice, whispering to one another as we scurried around behind the scenes, battling our way through the thick haze of cigarette smoke.

This is not to say that I don't have wonderful memories of being with my father. One of my favourites is of him on New Year's Eve. I grew up being told that Italians have a superstition that wearing red underwear on New Year's Eve will guarantee good luck in the coming year. For 99.99 percent of us, this means first putting on our red underwear, then our outer garments before heading out for the evening's festivities. For my dad, it meant wearing red underwear outside his pants. He was always looking for ways to liven up the party. The more outrageous, the better. He loved catching people off guard and making them laugh. The chances are good that if you and my dad were at the same party, you would remember the night, thanks to him.

As was true in every close relationship I had in my life, there was also a flip side to the happy memories and good feelings I have for my parents. There were instances that I considered pivotal in my life because they showed me how out of balance I was when it came to my identity and self-confidence. One of my earliest memories of this feeling of insignificance was the first time I met my cousin Daniela when I was five years old.

We were expecting visitors from Italy who were going to spend time with us, and our house was filled with great excitement. My excitement was extinguished when the visitors arrived and I was introduced to a young girl about my age called by the same name. She was to share my room and sleep in *my* bed. Naturally, as a visitor in our home, she became the focus of attention and I was lost in the shuffle. I felt that I was no longer unique. I was replaceable, therefore insignificant.

It was easy to feel lost in the shuffle. Gatherings with our aunts, uncles, cousins and close family friends were very common. If we weren't gathering as a family, we were celebrating with family and friends, attending and hosting countless events, often business-related events. On one occasion when I was no more than six, my sisters and I were sent to bed while my parents were hosting a party in our home. After I was tucked in, one of my sisters came to me and told me that I had been called to go downstairs. I have no idea why she did this, yet I obeyed and went down to see what my parents wanted. My father saw me standing at the bottom of the stairs and became furious. He grabbed me by the shoulder, spun me around, spanked my butt and ordered me back upstairs with a very stern tone. These were the days when children were to be seen and not heard. In this instance, I was not to be seen either. I still remember the red handprint on my behind and the bruise on my tender heart.

I was quite shaken by this moment and the realization that following a trusted person's instructions and doing something so innocent as going downstairs could put me into such a painful predicament. Even when I was doing the right thing, I could still be accused of doing something awful. This incident would serve as just one of the many times in my life when I took the blame and carried the burden for something I didn't do. This moment was also the first time I realized that my dad could have a temper. I made it my mission never to cross him again. Still, my heart is filled with little tidbits of childhood memories of him making me smile more often than he made me cry.

My parents encouraged us to adopt their family traditions as part of our routines. As a child I was taught that when I enter someone's house, I greet every person individually. The Italian way was to give a kiss on each cheek. Anytime I entered my aunts' and uncles' houses, I went to each adult and said hello with a kiss even though I didn't really want to be pinched on the cheek by all those elders or feel the numerous greasy cheeks against mine. Alas, it was my duty, so I did it.

I believe I was coming into my twelfth year when one afternoon I walked into my aunt's house and went down to the basement to greet everyone there. I was going around kissing everybody when all of a sudden, my mother stormed up, pulled me away to the bathroom, closed the door and slapped me. She whispered angrily, "Why did you kiss that boy?"

"Boy?" I replied, confused. "I just went to greet everyone like you told me to."

At that, she turned and left me in the bathroom with no further explanation. I was devastated. I'd been taught to kiss everyone, and now it was not right to do so? Why? One moment yes, the next no. What was right and what was wrong? So many contradictions! It was a few years later, after I'd matured a little, that I figured it out. I was going through puberty, and I'd kissed a male who was around eighteen years old. To me, I was simply greeting an elder in my aunt's house; to my mother I was kissing an older boy. She never explained to me that things had changed because I was changing.

There was also a strong culture to be respectable children. We were taught to acknowledge our elders; look people in the eye when addressing them; not interrupt; use our manners and always be polite; understand that "No" means no, no questions asked; help others when a need arises and never be in a situation where rumors can be started.

The kissing incident was potentially one such situation. This was also one example of my mother creating contradictions that I found impossible to rationalize without her explaining a conflict or hardship to me so I could understand what was going on around me. On the other hand, I didn't consider the pressure my father must have put on her to keep their five daughters safe and out of trouble and free from local gossip.

My parents had picked up many of their traits from their own parents, who were also a valued presence in my life.

My family gathered for Lydia's First Communion and Sabrina's baptism, Montreal, 1973. Back, L–R, my father, Franco; Nonna Maria; my mother, Lia; Nonno Giuseppe; Nonna Enza, and Nonno Vincenzo. Front, L–R: Virginia, Lydia, Danielle, Sabrina and Patricia.

TREASURED ELDERS

The best classroom in the world is at
the feet of an elderly person.
—Andy Rooney

Giuseppe, my paternal grandfather who started the cheese company, was a jovial man. He was always active, always moving and always doing. I have lovely memories of him arriving at our home for visits. As soon as I saw his big car coming down our driveway, I would run out to greet him with great excitement because I knew that when Nonno Giuseppe entered the house, good things were soon to follow. He gave me attention, although short-lived, and what little girl doesn't crave attention? Being with him was such a delight. If I could have flown out the door to meet his car instead of running, I would have. I would stand in the driveway while he parked his car, eyes wide in anticipation of what was to come. He would emerge with a wide smile holding a paper bag full of candy—most often big chocolate bars—and would invite me to put my hand in and pull out a treat. A sweet gift and kind words directed just to me by my notable grandparent—what a delicious joy! My Nonno Giuseppe was there to please. From him, I learned the power of giving. He was a big, beautiful presence in my life.

Sadly, he was also my first experience with loss. I was sitting in an elementary school classroom one day when a school staff member appeared in the doorway, asking me to go with her to the principal's office. There, I was given the news that my dear Nonno Giuseppe had died. I shall never forget that feeling of absolute grief and utter confusion. My memories brought me to the days when he had been so full of life. Understanding that I would never again hear his merry voice or see his smile or feel the comfort of his embrace devastated me. This new reality left me numb with such sorrow that I was rendered tearless.

The saving grace in all this was my grandmother, Giuseppe's wife, Maria. She was the glue that kept the family together both before and after my grandfather's passing. Nonna Maria was the life of the party. From her I learned the power of documenting memories through photography and the coming together of family. She always had a camera in hand to record every event.

Even with all the good memories I have of her, there was one interaction between us that rather tinged the way I looked at her from then on. A male relative from my mother's side of the family had come to town for a visit, and Nonna Maria hadn't been told about it in advance. When she saw this relative, she turned to me and my younger sister, Sabrina, glared at us in disapproval and said, "You could have told me he was here! Why didn't you tell me?"

I could not believe she was trying to blame us. Although I knew my grandmother could not be serious about putting the fault on a young teenager, I took the blame anyway. This was just part of the cycle of shrinking ever further into the shadows, not knowing what would set off a family elder when I didn't meet their expectations. These small actions eroded my confidence, and I tried even harder to please those around me.

On the other side of my family tree, I spent hours of quality time with my maternal grandparents, Vincenzo and Enza, even though they moved around a lot. They retained a home in Sicily and spent much of their time in the United States, where their son, my uncle Vince, lived in Michigan, then later Florida. They also spent summer months with us in Canada. Nonno Vincenzo was a quiet individual with so much to teach. He had short salt-and-pepper hair and a long face with high defined cheekbones. His was a face covered with wrinkles of wisdom. I remember him as a tall man, although that could be because I was so small as a young girl. Nonno Vincenzo was my resident philosopher. If I had any questions about life, I could turn to him for the answers.

From him I learned to be curious and present in the moment and to relish a love of learning. He was incredibly involved and interactive with my sisters and me. He was artistic, articulate and great with his hands. He carved wood into intricate pieces of art. He molded clay into fun figurines. He transformed tin cans and our broken Barbie doll parts into medieval knights that he attached to strings and used them to create a marionette show. I remember him playing card games with us at the table in my parents' living room with his espresso and a cigarette. He was the only person in my life that I didn't mind smoking around me. I would even pick up the butts that remained from his unfiltered cigarettes and pretend to smoke them. (These, along with powdered bubble gum sticks rolled in paper and Popeye candy cigarettes, were the extent of my smoking.) Through these games, Nonno Vincenzo would teach us math and lessons in life. There was one game he loved to play with us called Sciccareddu, which is Sicilian for donkey. It's like a Sicilian version of Old Maid. Whoever was left with the last card would receive a playful tap on the arm and an infectious smile from Nonno Vincenzo as he called out, "Sciccareddu!" To me, he was magical—a model individual with a beautiful depth of presence.

His wife, my maternal grandmother, Nonna Enza, was somewhat of an enigma. She had dark eyes and dark hair, was barely five feet tall and had an infectious smile. I saw her as a strong, independent female figure, yet at the same time she constantly spoke of the need for women to demand the highest level of chivalry from men at all times. Whenever she spoke to me, she emphasized the importance of my appearance as I moved around in the world and in our home. She expected us to look our best because she believed that a proper appearance would gain us respect, and that was the one thing she wanted most for us. I had flat feet as a youngster, so I wasn't comfortable in high heels. Nonna Enza would always stop me and point out the crime of my wearing sensible, comfortable (and in her view, ugly) shoes. Even though she suffered with bunions and her feet were cramped and sore in heels, she wore them anyway. As she put it, ladies must learn to surpass the struggles and overcome pain in order to bring forth their beauty. Even as an octogenarian, she continued to wear a restricting corset.

She stayed overnight with me on a trip home from Italy after I had moved to Windsor, Ontario, in 2001. I was in my thirties. When I picked her up at the Detroit airport, a porter rolled her out to me in a wheelchair. I admired her for being so open to accepting help. Back at my house, she asked me to assist her with her bath and we experienced a great sense of connection as I helped her wash. There were numerous times I helped her clip up her corset. Every time she turned to me for assistance was another opportunity for our bond to deepen. From Nonna Enza I learned the power of sharing my vulnerabilities and owning myself with a great sense of courage—reaching out and connecting was the most beautiful thing.

I know she would be disappointed to see me running around in yoga pants and sneakers today. I also think she'd be pleased with my independence, which I believe I inherited from her. After Nonno Vincenzo passed away, Nonna Enza lived independently for many years. Two things I remember her always having in her purse were Wrigley's spearmint gum and an embroidered handkerchief. She was rarely without her knitting needles and a skein of wool. I recall her ending almost every sentence by asking, "H'ai capito?" (Do you understand?) She always had something to say, and I deeply felt her words were spoken with my best interests in mind.

And finally, I recall the glory of Nonna Enza's cooking. She was masterful in the kitchen, just like my mom. On one of my grandparents' summer visits to our home, Nonna Enza's sister, Zia Pina, who lived in Michigan, came too. I loved watching the two sisters giggling, rolling macaroni, spending hours just for the love of making meals for the family. Believe me when I say that you could taste the love in every delicious bite.

For the majority of my life, the talk at home and at our many large family gatherings was focused on the business and the prosperity it had brought to all of us. This continued until some changes in the company took place before and into the early 2000s, which created a disconnect that remains even now. The company went public in 1997, and in the years that followed, many family members stopped working there and the company was run by one branch of the family. The business was no longer part of the family—at least not in the same way it was when I was growing up, which makes reminiscing about my childhood ever more bittersweet. Life was exceptionally good for me. I was loved and nurtured by my parents, my four sisters, my grandparents and my large extended family of aunts, uncles and cousins. At the centre of every family get-together was fabulous Italian food, and at the head of every table (figuratively and literally) were my grandparents. All four of them are gone now. To this day, thinking of them leaves me with a calming peace. They were wonderful people.

If I had to sum up these four elders—Giuseppe, Maria, Vincenzo and Enza—I would say that their greatest gift to me was a deep sense of family. They were like the hub of the wheel, the centre of all we did. When they were around, the whole family was around. They loved their family more than anything—more than the cheese company and all it brought us, more than the motherland of Sicily, which seemed so far away, and more than life itself. They passed that love through the generations with the greatest of care. I intend to pass this culture of love and family on to the best of my ability too, to honour their legacy.

While there was an abundance of love within our family, there was also a distinct sense that the elders' branches extended overhead, protecting us from the outside world. That shadow could, at times, hold back our own growth and keep us in the shade, tethered close to the trunk by our ancestors' values and decisions.

EARLY DEFINING MOMENTS

*Any person capable of angering you becomes
your master; he can anger you only when you
permit yourself to be disturbed by him.*
— *Epictetus*

As I've described, everything around me was good when I was growing up. I pretty much had it all. I came from a great family, lived in a wonderful neighbourhood, had superb friends and attended fabulous schools. I was a happy-go-lucky child even though I wasn't part of the popular group at school and was the quiet type. Although I had four sisters and seventeen first cousins, I spent a lot of time alone. My three eldest sisters, Virginia, Lydia and Patricia, are close in age, with only a year and a half between each other. Then there is a three-and-a-half-year gap between Patricia and me, leaving a ten-year gap between Virginia, the eldest, and Sabrina, the youngest of the five sisters. I was considered too young to hang out with my older sisters and our cousins, yet I didn't feel quite right going along with my baby sister Sabrina and the younger cousins.

That four-year age gap felt large when I was a young girl. From the time I was very young, whether the occasion was a wedding, a dinner or any of the other large Italian family gatherings, I'd find myself very often alone at a table set for ten. I didn't have my little tribe to run off with. That was okay with me. Being part of the crowd was never really my scene. I loved staying behind and having the house to myself when my parents and sisters went out. I'd pull out my quilting or put on a movie or read since I cherished those quiet moments.

As an introvert, I've preferred one-on-one relationships. I think that's why I was (and continue to be) very sensitive to people who are alone. When I would see someone alone at school, that's the person I would gravitate towards. As soon as they made new friends and didn't "need" me anymore, I'd move on to the next person I saw standing alone. This constant shuffling around and not connecting deeply often made me wonder where I belonged.

It's reflecting on these moments that now make me see how I created a story about myself. The following paragraphs describe other defining moments that enforced my false beliefs.

Frozen in the Spotlight

> We need to believe in ourselves because
> no one can do that for you.
>
> — Nokx Majozi

Being frozen in the spotlight occurred when I was in the third grade, as many of my classmates put together skits for the up-coming Christmas variety show. My friend Jackie approached me a few days before the show, desperate for help. She and another classmate had planned to perform the song "Rockin' Around the Christmas Tree," but the other girl had fallen ill and wasn't going to be able to attend. My friend pleaded with me to come to the rescue.

"Danielle, I really want to be in the show," she said. "Please, please, please be my partner and do the song with me!"

Oh, boy! A friend in need! I didn't even think twice. I told her I'd be happy to help her out. For the next several days she and I spent every lunchtime and recess practicing our skit. Unfortunately, remembering song lyrics was not one of my strengths, so I worked hard to learn all the words to the song. On the day of the program, we were so excited. We just knew that we were going to steal the show.

At last, it was our turn to perform. We took the stage and the bright spotlight hit me, and—I froze. I froze solid, like a tiny icicle, and all the words to the song escaped me. I felt as if all the air had been sucked from the room and the blood had drained from my body. I could no longer hear or speak. I just stood there in the white heat of the spotlight looking out at the full house. I could see a vast sea of dark heads, the silhouettes of all those people staring at me. My little friend beside me became so distraught about me ruining her skit that she ran off the stage in tears and locked herself in the bathroom. She wouldn't let me in to explain or apologize. It broke my heart to think I'd let her down. I felt such intense shame at having disappointed her, at having embarrassed my friend and myself. I believe that's why being in the spotlight has never been my thing. I also think that was the first time I publicly felt as if I wasn't good enough.

Close Call on My Commute

> *It is not the strongest of the species that*
> *survives, nor the most intelligent. It is the*
> *one that is most adaptable to change.*
>
> — *Charles Darwin*

In the Quebec school system, elementary school went to grade six, then high school started in grade seven. Going to a private high school in downtown Montreal represented a lifestyle change for me, mostly because I had to wake up so early and navigate the transportation system in order to get there. We lived an hour-and-a-half commute away from that school, and I had to wake up at 5:15 in the morning to catch a 6:15 train. Upon arrival in the city an hour later, I'd walk through the downtown core to make it to my first class at 8:00 a.m. I was lucky enough my first year to have my older sister Patricia, who was in her final year of high school, map out the roads for me. Patricia found ways to show me the landmarks so that I would not forget them and helped me memorize the streets of downtown Montreal. She taught me bus and metro routes in a fun, practical way to get me safely to and from school. All my sisters have given me precious gifts throughout our lives together. To Patricia, I owe a huge debt of gratitude for instilling in me a love of learning and for kick-starting the development of my street smarts.

After she graduated, I was on my own.

Having had a full year with my big sister by my side, I coped just fine on those long daily trips. It was a good growing experience for me. I had to learn to make decisions on the fly and jostle my way through teeming crowds of people much larger than me. I was exposed to many things that a downtown core had to offer, and I accepted them with wonder. I got to see early-morning delivery trucks unloading goods at restaurants representing cultures from all around the world and newsstands receiving their morning papers. Homeless people on street corners and in the underground metro stations begged for money, tourists asked for directions, businesspeople hustled to and from the numerous office buildings. The bicycle couriers wove in and out of traffic and came so close to the bus and taxi drivers, none of whom seemed to pay any attention to them. It was an environment of "survival of the fittest."

It was in downtown Montreal that I saw my first cellular phone in 1983, a large Motorola device with the word CANTEL written on it. It was odd watching this man walk down the sidewalk speaking out loud to what looked like no one. Upon closer inspection, I realized he was communicating into this weird contraption. It reminded me of the old war movies when soldiers in the trenches used satellite telephones to call for help. Why would anyone want to conduct their office affairs in the street? I wondered. Little did I know where this new technology would take us in just a few short years.

One of my best memories of my daily trek through downtown Montreal was of the Halloween morning when I was thirteen. Halloween was my favourite day of the year, and I usually went all out when it came to decorations and costumes. On this day I dressed up as Pierrot—the sad clown or mime with a white-painted face and a big black teardrop rolling down one cheek. I boarded the train in costume, and although Pierrot was supposed to be sad, I could not help smiling from ear to ear.

Returning home after school, still in costume, I was walking towards the train station along the busy street of Saint Catherine when in front of me, I saw a man holding a little girl who was crying. I met the pace the pair were walking and assumed the role of a silent clown. Once I had the little girl's attention, I pointed at my painted tear with a frown, then pointed to her and changed my frown to a smile. Oh, the power of a smile! The girl lit up with a grin so bright, I still remember it more than thirty-seven years later. I knew I was dressed that way for a reason, and that moment was it. She made my day. I had passed hundreds if not thousands of people that morning and afternoon, and many heads turned as I walked by. All the perplexed stares I'd endured were well worth that one smile.

That's just one of the many gifts I gained from my daily travels to school. My ability to see beyond what was in front of me became fine-tuned during those five years between the ages of twelve and seventeen. It was then that I gained the courage to try new things.

Not all of my commutes led to happy memories. One afternoon when I was around fourteen, I fell asleep on the train while returning home from school. For some reason I was not awakened by the conductor who usually came by to check my pass. When I finally woke up, it took me a moment to realize that I was alone on a train that was not moving. I looked out the window and saw a station I did not recognize. All I knew for sure was that this was neither my station in Laval-sur-le-Lac nor any of the stations I was accustomed to seeing on my way home every day. I waited a few minutes to see if a conductor would appear. No one came.

With great hesitation I gathered my gym bag, clarinet case and school bag and stepped off the train to look for clues about my location. A sign on the station wall informed me that I was at the end of the line in Lake of Two Mountains, which was the stop after Laval-sur-le-Lac. I had never been there before. Thinking that only one stop away from my home station couldn't be that far, I made the fateful decision to walk back to Laval-sur-le-Lac along the train tracks rather than wait an hour until the next train.

The trek started easily enough, until I came to a fairly daunting obstacle: the railway bridge that connects the two stations that had no pedestrian walkway. What do I do now? I wondered. Do I cross this bridge over the icy water with my hands full of bags, never having done this before? I considered turning back and waiting for the next train headed to Laval-sur-le-Lac, yet the pressure of getting home on time for supper was weighing on me. If I were late, I would upset my parents and I certainly didn't want to do that. I set out across the bridge, with the courage I'd built over the last year, step by careful step along the iron rail. I didn't want to lose my footing because the space between the wooden planks was large enough for me to fall through and the water below was far from inviting. I didn't dare look down. I kept my eyes on my destination—the solid ground at the end of the bridge—and slowly made my way across, all the while thinking how crazy this was.

Crazier yet was when I felt the rails start to vibrate. I stopped walking and glanced over my shoulder to see a bright light shining behind me. What the ... ? Then I heard the loud blast of a train horn. A train was coming!

There was no place for me to step off. The only way out was forward, and I wasn't sure if it was possible to make it to the end before the train hit me. To this day I have never been more terrified than I was in that moment. It was amazing what adrenaline can do. My heart was beating in my throat, and I broke out in a cold sweat. It felt as if all my senses had been cranked up to the highest spot on the dial. Every sensation, every sound, sight and smell were magnified. Every breath was more deliberate than the last. Even though it was daylight, I felt as if I were inside a dark tunnel and the only thing I could see was my salvation at the end of the bridge.

In genuine fear for my life, I picked up the pace and put one foot in front of the other, teetering along while balancing my bags and doing all I could to keep panic at bay. The train horn bellowed behind me again, much closer this time. I was so close to the end and not quite there yet. At this point, I did not dare look back. I was entirely focused on where I needed to be—off the track. I was going to have to run for it. I summoned my courage, took a deep breath and made three final leaping strides forward, vaulting my body off the tracks mere seconds before being pushed by the force of the accelerating train. I did not turn to look at it. I did not want to face the demon that almost took my life. Every train car that passed whispered wickedly in its clickety-clack and iron-against-iron screeches, "Almost got you, almost got you, almost got you!" Only when the train had completely passed could I bring myself to turn my head. Shaking and chilled to the soul, I gathered my courage and resumed my walk.

I did all this to make it home on time and not disappoint my parents. I would have chosen to be hit by a train rather than let down my mom and dad. My only focus as a child was to please my parents. In my mind, I was not an autonomous person. I was insignificant beyond my place in the family they had created. Serving them was the only thing I cared about. From cleaning my room, vacuuming the house, sweeping the outside driveway and granite walkway until my hands blistered, making breakfast for the family on weekends, preparing my parents' bed at night, cleaning up after my pets, bringing home good marks, having others speak well of me, continuing my education beyond high school and living at home with them until the age of thirty: all this was done to satisfy my mother and father.

In return, I lived comfortably in the shadow of our large family tree. It provided all I needed except seeing myself as an individual and feeding my inner self to achieve life's fullest fulfillment. That tree provided great support except the ability to fully shine as me. Giving my parents every reason to be happy and proud of me was my full-time job. I had no thoughts of expanding myself for my own sake or living my life to its fullest potential. I was fully one-sided on the paradox of autonomy or family. I did not have the wisdom then to know a state of fulfillment is achieved when it is both-and. Finding my autonomy was most fulfilling *and* made me a greater asset to the family.

A New Girl with a Big Question

> *Never change who you are so that other people*
> *will like you. Just be yourself and the right*
> *people will love you just for being you.*
>
> — *Unknown*

Once I'd mastered the logistics of my daily trek, high school was fun. I was involved in sports and had a great group of friends that I treasured, friends that I have to this day. By tenth grade, I was on top of the world. Everything in my life was secure and happy until the New Girl arrived. I was at my locker gathering my books one morning when a new student with a locker next to mine turned to me with a smile and said something out of the blue and puzzling: "Wow, Danielle, it must be difficult being you."

Difficult being me? Nobody had ever said anything like that to me before. It made no sense. I had a great family and no hardships to speak of. Yeah, I had to wake up early every morning, and that was no big deal. Confused, I asked her what she meant.

"I mean, how do you know who your real friends are and who is only hanging around with you because of your famous last name?" she replied.

I was baffled. It had never dawned on me that someone might want to be around me only because my name is Saputo. My mind started spinning. Was this something I should have been thinking about all along? My parents had never told me I had to worry about it, nor had my sisters, aunts or uncles. If it had been important, they would have warned me, right? Oh my gosh, maybe I was naïve!

Looking back, I don't believe the girl was asking me that question to hurt me, she asked simply out of curiosity. I don't think she realized the effect such a question would have on me as a teen and throughout my life. The question became a pivotal moment in my life. From that moment, I began to look at people differently. I began to question the validity of all my relationships outside the family, including my classmates, sports teammates, neighbours, even my teachers. Did they really like me, or were they only pretending? What were they really after? Instead of thinking about the exciting questions I needed to answer at that stage of my life—questions like which university I would attend and what I would study—I became consumed with the question of whether people's attention to me was sincere. What were their motives for befriending me? My happy-go-lucky nature stalled, and my trust in people plummeted.

Whenever I was asked the simple question, "What's your name?" I paused. The answer never seemed simple again. I began introducing myself as Danielle. "Danielle who?" they would ask. I would reply with a resolute "Danielle." This was not out of shame or lack of pride in my family name. It arose from a growing fear that I would be taken advantage of in the responsive ignorance of others who would treat me differently. Later in life, this carried over to my relationships with money managers, bankers, lawyers and all the other professionals I had to deal with, including salespeople and real estate brokers. I was afraid that the price would be marked higher and the negotiations would not be fair because my name is Saputo. In other words, I was stripped of my belief that whoever crossed my path was there for a legitimate reason and authentically showing interest in me. That lack of trust would make me feel terribly sad and alone.

Lessons About Dollars and Sense

No regrets in life. Just lessons learned.

— Unknown

When I was fourteen, my father took early retirement from the family business after decades of hard work. Shortly after we moved north from Montreal to Laval, my dad's siblings gifted him with a boat and, consequently, my parents, sisters and I spent many happy weekends boating together. I felt so at home on the water. I could spend hours watching the waves, dangling my feet over the edge as I sat at the front of our eight-seater boat. From the marina in Laval-sur-le-Lac, we would cross Lake of Two Mountains all the way to a quaint area called Sainte-Anne-de-Bellevue. We would dock before the locks, disembark and spend the afternoon enjoying every moment. We would eat pizza and ice cream and stroll around, then return to the boat and make our way home. These are the memories I always return to when I think of our most precious family time. Not only was I my dad's first mate, untying and tying the boat at the docks, this was also a shared adventure with my parents, my sisters and the numerous guests my dad invited along for a ride. We had such a wonderful time together with many smiles, much laughter and the satisfaction of a day well spent.

Although my dad would still go to the office from time to time, it was upon his retirement that he became a steady presence in the house and I got to discover who he really was. My dad loved auto mechanics and had a handsome car collection. I spent many happy hours standing beside him as he tinkered under the hoods of those cars. Through him, I learned the names of his tools and their uses. Because he was so mechanically inclined, he was Mr. Fix-It inside the house as well. Whenever some household item broke—be it the clothes dryer, the refrigerator or the coffee machine—he'd take it apart, find what was wrong, get it working again and put it back together. I loved being his assistant on many of these do-it-yourself projects. I think that's what led me to be so hands-on in my own home and life as an adult. If something wasn't working and there was any way I could fix it myself, I did. I have my dad to thank for that.

His projects taught me about much more than just tools and mechanics. They also were an early lesson in the value of money. My father had the means to pay for virtually any repair job you can imagine, yet he chose to do them himself—and not just because he enjoyed tinkering. It was also because he did not like to spend money. Through him, I learned that money did not grow on trees; in fact, it was a very rare crop indeed. Whenever I approached my dad for anything on the financial side—for cash, funds for a class trip or even school supplies—he didn't give me an easy time of it. When I was in high school, he gave me an allowance of $100 a month—which sounds like a lot for a young teen of that era—with a catch: he also made me responsible for purchasing my own monthly train pass to get to and from school, at a cost of $95. When I joined the soccer team and asked for money for cleats and other sports equipment, he said, "No. You're given $100 a month and that's it. Do what you gotta do."

My father's stubbornness with money thus turned me into a wise little budgeter and saver. As my birthday money rolled in or the aunts gave me an extra token here and there, I hoarded it all because I knew that I had expenses to cover, if not that day, then soon. Being born into a family of affluence didn't mean my pockets were lined with $100 bills. I learned at an early age that I had to work smart to accumulate my own funds. Sometimes things didn't work out with my budgeting despite my best efforts. At a party at my uncle's home, I received some cash gifts from my aunts. I held onto the money tightly throughout the evening since I wasn't carrying a purse at the time. At one point, I had to go to the bathroom and I placed my treasured gifts on the toilet tank and did what I had to do. I washed my hands and returned to the party. Within minutes, I realized that I had forgotten to collect my cash. I ran back to retrieve it, only to find that it was gone. My treasure had become someone else's, and there was no way to get it back. I was angry with myself for being so careless. I was even angrier at the people around me. I was deeply disappointed to think that someone would take what was not theirs and claim it as their own. My innocent mind could not accept that there were people like that around me.

I experienced another loss at a track meet in high school. I thought that placing my bag far away from the crowd higher up on the bleachers would make it safer. I was wrong. Sometimes, blending into the crowd is the best action. My bag was one of a handful reported stolen, along with my monthly train pass money as well as a red Walkman (the loss of which I think about to this day). My father was not sympathetic. This taught me that money can easily be lost or stolen and that it had to be put in a safe place to be protected.

I was describing these childhood memories to a friend recently when she remarked that my dad's penny-pinching behaviour must have made me feel really frustrated and angry. While I can't say that I enjoyed it, I can't say that it made me angry either. I simply didn't know any different until I spent one eye-opening weekend with some cousins when I was a young teenager. We walked from their house to the *dépanneur* (a neighbourhood convenience store), and one of my younger cousins pulled out a $100 bill to buy a few cents' worth of candy. This was back when copper pennies still existed and had some value. I was stunned. Wow, I thought, she has $100 in her pocket to spend on candy while I'm counting my pennies to buy a train pass to get to school? It dawned on me that not everybody's father was teaching them the way mine was teaching me.

I had yet another hard lesson on money from my dad when he came across a beautiful secondhand white BMW black-top convertible through a friend of the family and thought it would be a great car for me. Little did I know that Dad's idea was that all my hard-earned savings would pay for this car. My funds plunged down to zero without a discussion, and the feeling of running on empty was far from energizing. I had been raised to believe that money meant freedom and security. Without it, one was neither free nor secure. Being broke scared me because I knew that if something came up and I needed money, I would not be able to ask my dad for help. I felt very much alone as I worked feverishly to restore my savings as quickly as possible. I learned that I never again wanted to feel what it had felt like to have no money in my account.

Despite the worry about my finances, I enjoyed the BMW for many years. It gave me a sense of autonomy. It was a safe space for all the hours I spent on the road when I worked at the family company visiting manufacturing plants in Trois Rivières and Maskinongé. It was my transport for adventure going from the Laurentian Mountains north of Montreal to the Eastern Townships on weekends and crossing the border to go shopping in Plattsburgh, New York, for quilting fabric and supplies.

Like my father, my mother also taught me the value of money. It was she who helped me open my first bank account. I loved watching the funds grow over the years. I recall those early years going to the bank making my first deposits with my mom, who guided me through the growth of my money and explained the importance of saving it.

Money lessons were some of the toughest lessons I had to learn as a teen. These well-appreciated, hard lessons made me financially savvy. My heart softens when I think of my parents going to such lengths to teach me how to manage money, one of the most important things a person can learn.

My heart also softens when I recall my father showing me his sensitive side. For so many years, he was under intense pressure, building the family business and providing for a wife and five daughters, while handling the stresses of being one of eight siblings. When he spoke with a harsh tone or slammed his hand down on the table in anger, I admit that I sometimes viewed him as a stern character. One day, he and I were working together in the garage, quietly going about some tinkering when out of the blue he turned to me and said, "Dani, you know that even though my voice might be rough sometimes, I have always loved you and I always will." I don't know what had happened to compel him to say that. Perhaps he'd had a disagreement with one of my sisters earlier in the day and had been hurt by it. All I know for sure was that in that moment, I realized my father did have a tender heart. It was the one and only time I ever saw such a display of affection. It is one of my sweetest memories.

While he dropped his guard with me that day, my mother kept her secrets to herself. When she was in her early forties, she was diagnosed with breast cancer. She kept this news to herself and shared nothing of it with me and my sisters, the oldest of whom was in her twenties and certainly mature enough to handle it. Instead, my mother went through the ordeal silently. Even when she'd lost all her hair and started wearing wigs, she went about her business as if everything were perfectly fine. My dad supported that approach. At the same time, we girls could see that something strange was happening in our house. Something was wrong, yet no one would acknowledge it. It was extremely confusing and isolating for me at the tender age of sixteen. That was the culture at the time. We lived in a closed world regardless of wealth. And there were definite ideas about propriety.

My mother stoically took all sufferings for herself and herself alone. When I was younger, I thought she and my dad were protecting us by keeping "bad" things from us, and now that I am a parent, I see it differently. Parents must share the bad as well as the good. That's how our children learn. I see strength in a mother showing her vulnerability. If vulnerabilities are not shared in moments like this, then I'm not helping my children grow. I'm going to send them out into the world with no concept of how to deal with difficult situations. Isn't it better for my children to learn how to handle difficulties with me by their side to comfort and guide them? I think so.

Still, I know my mother did the best she could with the knowledge and insights she had. Times were different. Saving face was important and part of the family culture. Knowledge was not at our fingertips as it is today. She was a delightful mom, and I enjoyed (and still enjoy) spending time with her. Being the last one to leave home gave me a different kind of relationship with her because it allowed us time with just the two of us. I had the opportunity to closely watch her cooking and to ask questions. We were also able to have conversations that didn't happen when my sisters were around. Being one-on-one allowed me to see my mother's perspective on things and use my voice to share my views.

Today she is still preparing meals for us, now with my dad at her side in the kitchen. They're lovely to watch as they put together family dinners on Sundays and holidays. As much as they may bicker, they're still so in tune with each other. From them, I have learned the value of money and achieving a great life/work balance. They have truly been an inspiration to me in every aspect of my life, most notably in my parenting.

While those benefits come upon reflection now, as a young woman, I was still consumed by how my actions represented my family. Compliance was the one task I could excel at better than anyone else. Unfortunately, my subservient approach to life only led to feelings of confusion, shame, inadequacy and invisibility. Every move I made and every word I spoke was scrutinized through the all-encompassing lens of what my parents would think, what they would say, what they would do and how my actions would make them look to the outside world.

It was not until I was in my twenties and met my first boyfriend that my attention occasionally turned to what might be best for me. He opened the door for me to question authority and shift my mindset ever so slightly from "serving them" to "serving me." He encouraged me to come out of the shadow of my large family tree and into the sunshine where I could be me.

The Sting of Distrust

> *The privilege of a lifetime is being who you are.*
> — Joseph Campbell

From high school, I went to Vanier College to complete my two years of CEGEP (General and Vocational College). There, I gained a new crop of friends, almost all of them boys. They were not boyfriends, simply male buddies. Coming from an all-girls school, the change was welcomed. I connected more easily with the guys, as communication flowed without judgment and the connection felt more real. We'd ski together, play racquetball and have conversations that fed the soul.

After college, I attended Concordia University in Montreal, where I earned a bachelor of commerce degree and a graduate degree in institutional administration. When I was studying there, I was chosen to attend a business conference that was taking place at nearby McGill University. I remember entering the conference room that day along with the handful of students like me who were invited to attend the event. The room was packed with professional people representing their businesses, all of them dressed in their finest office attire and exuding self-assurance. It was a little intimidating. I was standing off to the side, waiting for the seminar to begin and watching all these poised, confident people milling about, when I was approached by an older gentleman I did not know. He extended his hand, introduced himself and told me the name of his company.

"And who are you?" he asked with a friendly smile.

"Me? Oh, I'm just a student," I said.

"Just a student?" he replied, shaking his head. "No, you are much more than that! To be in this room with all these successful people, to be studying in university and earning a business degree? My dear, you are much more than 'just' a student. Never forget that!"

(This was another defining moment for me as you will see in the chapters ahead.)

Well, shucks, I thought. If I'm more than "just" a student, then who am I? I could not answer that question with any certainty. What I did know was that I was adding to my insignificance in the language I was using. "Just," and "but," are powerful words that create an image in the subconscious. Change my language, and I can change my outlook on who I am.

> *Words can inspire. And words can*
> *destroy. Choose yours well.*
>
> — *Robin Sharma*

My friend Tony and I ran the university's Entrepreneurs Association together, with him as president and me as vice president of finance. We were a great team working together through the Entrepreneurs Association, where we organized seminars and provided business planning tools. The office next to ours belonged to the Finance Association. I was seeking out my first wealth manager to help me invest some money, and the association was a wonderful resource. With their help, I found a good wealth manager, and after a few conversations, I opened my first account with a great Canadian bank.

These were exciting times. I felt in my element, and I loved the world of entrepreneurship and investment. Thus, when Tony and I heard about an upcoming entrepreneurship competition amongst the Canadian universities, we entered it. The judging was to take place at a three-day event at Queen's University in Kingston, Ontario, during which we had to present a case study and a business plan. The top three presentations would win a cash award to start up their businesses. We worked hard on our business plan, then travelled to Kingston and made our presentation with great enthusiasm. During the awards ceremony on the second day, we learned—much to our amazement—that we had been awarded second place. We were so proud of ourselves and eager to attend the big wrap-up party scheduled for the next day.

Upon returning to the hotel room on that second afternoon in Kingston, I was welcomed with a message that my mother had called. I returned the call, excited to tell her about our big win. She didn't want to hear it. She said that she had phoned the hotel's front desk to get my room number, only to learn that the room was in Tony's name. The idea that I was sharing a room with a male who was not my husband was a bridge too far for my mother. It was very much against the culture she grew up in, and she was furious. I tried to explain that we were in the same room because the university would pay for only one. We were sleeping in separate beds and Tony had a girlfriend, but Mom would not listen. She let me know exactly what she thought of me and what I'd done. She ended the call by ordering me home immediately. I was crushed to discover that my mother didn't trust me. Could she really be thinking what I thought she was thinking? How dare she devalue all the hard work I had done to get to where I was!

I have always been one to abide by the rules given to me. For example, when my parents said we had to sit through the meal and not get up until the end, I'd be a good little girl and sit there quietly until everyone was done with dessert. Some of these meals were seven-course dinners where I would often find myself sitting alone at a table set for ten, yet I never budged. Others at the table would dismiss themselves together (as a little tribe that I was not part of) to use the toilet and delay their return until the next dish was served. I didn't leave my seat until I received permission to. So, you know me, when Mom told me to come home that day, I did as I was told. I found Tony, handed him our prize cheque and told him to do whatever he wanted with it. I had to go home. He urged me to stay for the celebration, but I declined and drove three hours back to my parents' house.

Back home, my mother had no interest in hearing about my greatest success to date. It didn't matter to her that my work had beat out dozens of entrants from Canada's best universities. In her mind, I had put myself in a disgraceful situation where I could be the point of gossip and that was all she focused on. What should have been a wonderful moment was ruined. I felt completely devalued as a student, as a daughter, as a young woman and an entrepreneur. Unfortunately, this would not be the last time I felt the sting of my parents' distrust when it came to my blooming independence. Repeated moments like this kept me silent for many years. Whatever I had to say was dismissed and shut down. I was not being heard. I believed my voice did not matter.

Another incident arose with a friend named Eric. He and I met when we were both sales reps for Cutco, a kitchen supplies company. Our friendship deepened to a relationship when he sent me flowers to my workplace, picked me up unexpectedly and took me out to dinner. He then went to study in Sweden, and I spent an Easter vacation visiting him and touring Scandinavia while he was in classes. I began dreaming of a fairytale future with Eric, living in a cottage on a lake, believing all my dreams could come true. However, upon his return, he broke the news to me that he was gay. While that was the end of the romance, our friendship taught me how to dream and to move towards my goals one step at a time.

Eric had a cottage in eastern Quebec. One beautiful day when I was in my midtwenties, we went skiing with some other friends there. It was snowing lightly, which was no big deal; we were there to enjoy the winter wonderland. The snow was coming down a little heavier by the time I set out for home that evening. There was a long driveway leading from the cottage, and at the end was a little curve going up a hill towards a busy main street. Long story short, my car got stuck at the top of that driveway. I walked all the way back down to the cottage and called the guys out to give me a push. I had my trusty BMW with front-wheel drive, and the rear wheels were slipping and sliding while gaining no traction whatsoever. I ended up getting pushed deeper into the ditch, stuck even worse than I had been before. Eric knew of a guy with a 4×4 vehicle, so he called him. The plan was to tie my car to his truck so he could pull me out, but it didn't work. I was really stuck. We summoned a tow truck and settled in for a long wait.

Throughout this ordeal, I was calling my parents every half hour to keep them up to date on my progress (or lack thereof). Eventually, the tow truck arrived and pulled me out. The weather had worsened, and the light snow had turned into a blizzard. Having been out in the snow for so long, the cold and dampness had seeped through my winter wear and chilled me to the bone.

So—very innocently—I called my mother and suggested that perhaps it would be safer if I stayed at the cottage overnight and left in the morning, after the snowplows had had a chance to clear the roadways. Safety first, right?

"Are you kidding?" she said. "No way. You come home right now."

That was the worst drive I've ever taken in my life. Whether my eyes were open or closed, it made no difference. I was driving in whiteout conditions. Everything was just this deep blanket of white, and I had no idea where the sides of the road were or if I was even on the road anymore. My hands were gripping the steering wheel so tightly, my knuckles were as pale as a ghost. To summon whatever gods there may be out there, I kept repeating, "Please, road, be straight. Please, road, be straight. Please, road, be straight!"

It took me three horrifying hours to get home; a drive under ideal conditions would take half that time. By then, I was shaking in a way my body had never shaken before and my mom—who was quite angry with me—chose that moment to deliver a sentence I shall never forget: "Danielle, I gave you life and I can take it away." I couldn't believe my ears. I knew that I had worried my mother; however, she didn't stop to think for one second about what I'd just been through. That was my perception, since she spoke not a word that comforted me. We both let each other down in this situation, my mother and me.

I've learned in the last few years that moments like this create stories we then live by. Even in anger, I try not to spit out words that could sting for a lifetime, and if I do, it brings me back right to this moment with my mother. Now that I too am a mom and have a greater understanding of my mother's deep love and concern for me, I can feel gratitude for the lesson she taught me in that instance. I know for a fact that by saying such harsh words to me in the heat of the moment and by making me take blame and carry a burden that I didn't deserve, she was planting a seed that would help me become a gentler, more contemplative mother than I might otherwise have been. Despite the sting of hurt in the moment, I remain grateful and forgiving.

Another good friend represents a defining moment in my life. Lan and I shared a bond above and beyond the norm. From him I learned the power of connection and free-flowing communication. His openness and his ability to talk about everything imaginable was so enlightening. He carried a trust in others that I had long ago lost. With him, I found hope. Lan understood me like no one else. He had the uncanny ability to complete my every thought. It was so funny; he often spoke the words I was thinking just as the thought was formulating in my mind.

We both worked at my family company, Saputo Inc. By pure chance we would enter the office building at exactly the same moment almost every morning. It could not have been planned any better. As he showed greater interest in me, I told him I could not have a committed relationship with an employee of the family company. His response was to change careers, with the anticipation of having the chance to date me. I was profoundly moved by his commitment to me for just being me. We enjoyed each other's company very much and spent many happy hours hiking, watching movies and eating Vietnamese food. I was falling for him, and he was falling for me.

I was on a holiday in Florida with my parents when I confided in my mom about my new fellow. As she and I walked together on the beach, I told her of my concern that Lan, who is Vietnamese, wouldn't be accepted by the family. I was not sure about having a relationship with someone whose culture was different from ours. Yet, I explained to her, his good qualities were abundant, and his kindness, tenderness and respect towards me were like nothing I'd ever experienced. (Looking back, I realize I was "enough" in his eyes, which was refreshing and empowering.) My mother voiced no objection to my pursuing the relationship, so I assumed that meant she and my father would support it. I should have known better than to assume. The fact that they had no vocal objection did not mean that I had their full approval. Even the merest of mildly unkind comments from them would play over and over again in my head, and the perception of parental criticism became too great for me to bear. My relationship with Lan would not survive. Like it or not, I put family peace before all else. This sort of peace, however, has nothing to do with peace of mind or peace at heart. It was merely an absence of war.

Other Defining Moments

> *When a defining moment comes along, you define the moment, or the moment defines you.*
> — Kevin Costner

The struggle between feeling valued and respected by people outside the family circle, yet lacking confidence while inside the fold, continued. In fact, it became accentuated anew once I entered the Saputo business. After university, I went to work as a sales rep for the Cutco cutlery company in 1995. I was looking at a particular paring knife one day when it dawned on me that my family's company might be able to use them in the packaging department. I made a sales presentation to one of my cousins who ran a department at Saputo. While he didn't place an order for the knives, he did offer me a full-time job. I accepted and began working at Saputo Inc. in 1996.

At first, I was responsible for telecommunication systems, then the preparation for Y2K (the technology to update systems to dates reflecting the impending new century) and security at the head office. Later, I was made responsible for selling buildings that were no longer used and vacated. Over the course of my first year there, I began dealing with more and more sales reps. They would give me their business cards and ask for mine, except I didn't have one. I spoke to my cousin for permission to have business cards printed up, and he hesitated. I'm not sure why exactly, so I came up with two possible reasons. First, they didn't want to promote the fact that I was a Saputo, and the second reason was that they didn't know what job title to put on my card. It was quite a blow to realize that I'd been working for the company for a year, and my superiors didn't even know how to identify me.

Eventually, they did supply me with business cards, with the job title of "Administrative Assistant." My interpretation was that I wasn't worthy of having a card reflecting my actual tasks or the name Saputo. I wondered, Who am I to wear such a badge of honour, to be an official part of something so big, so successful, so reputable as my family's company? It was a crushing experience. I now know to answer, "Who am I *not* to?" (as I learned from Marianne Williamson's quote seen earlier). I didn't have that wisdom at the time.

On the upside, the support of two of my eldest sisters who had been working for some time at the family company really buoyed me during this phase of my life. Lydia and I carpooled together when working at Saputo for a time, and I will always remember her willingness to lend a helping hand. Her lunch hours were often spent helping a co-worker out of one bind or another. Never too proud to admit her own shortcomings or personal difficulties, Lydia was open to sharing her hardships if she felt it would benefit the other person. She's the poster child for generosity, giving freely without expecting anything in return. I would see her tip liberally those who provided her with service at a restaurant, a hotel or a service station. Lydia hasn't overlooked a kindness done towards her, and she rewards it from the bottom of her heart. From her I learned the power of selfless giving.

Virginia, the eldest and the most jubilant one, didn't miss an opportunity to make merry. She didn't always act within society's limitations or stay safely in her lane. She could easily be called outspoken. She was uninhibited, spontaneous and untamed. From her, I inherited one of the great joys of my life, which is a love of motorcycle riding.

For many years before, throughout my high school years, Virginia's 450cc Honda motorcycle sat idle in my parents' garage. It was a beautiful piece of machinery that sparked my curiosity. I thought it was such a shame to have it sitting unused, so Sabrina, my youngest sister, and I decided to learn how to ride. After taking lessons, passing the road test and achieving the coveted capital M on our driver's licenses, we asked our dad if he would get Virginia's old bike running for us. He was surprised that we had gone through the process of learning to ride and without hesitation started up Virginia's motorcycle.

I had great fun riding that Honda and became determined to have a bike of my own. I scoured the work ads in the newspaper to find a job to raise the money to buy one. Actually, I had several jobs that summer: selling Cutco knives (both by referral and by going door-to-door) as well as promoting Lipton and Ocean Spray products by providing samples outside a variety of grocery stores. Talk about pushing myself outside my comfort zone.

I wanted that bike! I made enough money that summer to pay cash for my motorcycle, a 1100cc Yamaha Virago. I still have it to this day. It serves as a reminder of how hard I worked to put money aside to fulfill a dream. Hard work pays off.

My best ride to date was on my birthday in 1997. I left early that morning with a group of riders; there were at least eighteen of us if not more. There's something special about riding in such a group. I may have been one of the youngest riders and at the time the only female riding alone. Two older gentlemen took me under their wings during the trip. They had me ride between them and taught me formation and the rules of the road for riding in a pack. We travelled scenic roads from Laval through Montreal to Saint-Jean-sur-Richelieu, across the US border to the mountains of Vermont. In one day, I rode through what felt like all four seasons: a cold morning, then a little rain followed by the heat of the afternoon sun, and finally, crisp snow in the mountains. I sang as I rode along and enjoyed each moment. I arrived a little late to my birthday supper, and it was worth it.

I often rode my motorcycle to work at Saputo, leaving home dressed in leather, feeling free as a bird and capable of conquering anything that would come my way. I would park in the underground parking at the office—a privilege of being family—and change before anyone saw me. Then I would walk to my desk like a changed person. I would perform all my tasks to perfection but have that inner voice that whispered, "You are not seen."

I don't ride as much today, yet when I do, I give myself the luxury of taking time just for me. I love to ride as the sun begins to set. I have Virginia to thank for the joyful inspiration. From her I learned that when I'm comfortable with myself, my joy and happiness are contagious.

Returning home on my 1996 Yamaha Virago after a Sunday brunch with family and friends at Château Vaudreuil, Montreal, September 1997.

Part 2—Creating My Own Legacy

FOLLOWING MY HEART

Joy is a decision, a really brave one, about
how you are going to respond to life.
—Wess Stafford

One afternoon in 1989 when I was in my late teens, I was doing laps in my parents' swimming pool when I saw, standing by the pool ladder, a curious man I did not know. He was beckoning me with his eyes to come over to him. I had just gotten home from a hectic day at school and needed to do my laps to help me relax and unwind, so I ignored him and kept on swimming. The next time I came up for air, he was still there. I swam over to him. He introduced himself as Corrado Geloso, the son of family friends from the old village in Sicily. He was studying medicine in Ontario and had come to Montreal to attend a medical conference at McGill University. Since he was in town, he had stopped by my parents' home to pay his respects, as was the Italian way when there's some kind of relation between the families.

I greeted him and thought, Just because he's a doctor he thinks I'm going to drop everything and converse with him? I told him that it was nice to meet him, wished him a good day, turned around and resumed my laps. He stayed for dinner and spent the evening with my family before returning home.

Ten years later, in my late twenties, my Nonna Enza, by then a widow, announced that she wanted to return to Italy and would love for one of her grandchildren to accompany her. Since she was not getting any younger, I wanted to spend as much time with her as I could. Going to Italy with her sounded like a fabulous way to deepen our bond. I could also connect with our extended family and experience the Sicilian culture firsthand. I made the arrangements to take time away from work, and off we went.

A day or two after our arrival in Sicily, Nonna Enza informed me that we were about to have some visitors. Nonna's goddaughter and her husband, who lived in the next town, were on their way. Nonna's sister Zia Pina and I spent a lovely day with the couple. Much of the visit was devoted to talking about their eldest son, who was living in Canada where he was practicing medicine. You guessed it—the man they were talking about was Corrado Geloso.

The story goes that the minute the couple returned home from the visit, they called their son in Ontario and told him to get to Sicily immediately because Enza's granddaughter Danielle was there. Somehow Corrado was able to take off from his duties for five days and fly to Sicily. We were re-introduced and enjoyed a beautiful time getting to know each other. Nonna Enza and I attended his grandmother's eighty-fifth birthday gathering, and I saw the way Corrado behaved around his family. It appeared that he didn't come to Sicily very often, because everyone was practically falling at his feet, gushing, "Oh, Corrado's here! The doctor's here!" As they clamored for his attention, I saw Corrado fully focused on each individual in front of him, giving them 100 percent of his attention in return. I thought, Hmm, maybe this is a pretty good guy here!

Nonna Enza and Zia Pina added to these positive thoughts for the duration of my stay in Sicily; two busy bees going about their chores, chiming in at every opportunity to tell me about all the good they saw in Corrado and his family. There was something quite precious about having these treasured elders plot out my future, speaking wise words and voicing lovely visions of all the good that would come to me if I were to join Corrado's family. I began to imagine the possibilities.

Zia Pina and Nonna Enza, Sicily, 1999.

On another day, Corrado came along when my uncle, Zio Pippo, and my treasured cousin Daniela—the one who shared my room during her visit from Italy when I was five—gave a tour of some of Sicily's historic cultural sites. We went to one spot I'll never forget, Agrigento's Valle dei Templi, where we saw the most beautiful mosaic ruins. Again, I was impressed with Corrado's attentiveness and his knowledge of Sicilian history and culture. Later that evening we went bowling and I got to see his fun and silly side. He made everyone laugh until our bellies hurt.

Later, he invited me to join him in buying fresh fish at the seafood market. I accepted his invitation and asked what time he would be picking me up.

"Well, it's a little difficult to say for sure," he said, "because the market only opens when the fishermen have returned to the docks. It can be anywhere from sunset to the wee hours of the morning. When I hear that the boats are coming in, I'll come get you."

And so, I waited. By eight o'clock, the sun had set, yet Corrado had still not arrived. Ten o'clock, still no Corrado. Midnight came and went. By one o'clock, I wondered if I should just head to bed. I asked my cousin and uncle, who were waiting up with me, what they thought, while expressing my discomfort at heading out at that late hour. Finally (mercifully!) at two o'clock in the morning, Corrado arrived and said the market would open at 3:00 a.m. We were off!

The fish market was like nothing I'd ever experienced. Although my parents are Sicilian and I have Sicilian blood, I understood nothing that was going on in that place. The air was filled with a strange chorus of shouting, whistles and throat clearing. People were waving their arms and winking at one another in weird ways, all serving as a system of negotiation between the buyers and sellers. I consider that trip to the fish market to be one of the greatest cultural experiences of my life. It also allowed me to break the belief my parents had instilled in me that only terrible things happen after midnight. There was a whole world awake at these wee hours, living life to the fullest, and it wasn't bad at all; it was fantastic!

Corrado was enchanted by my fascination with the whole scene, so much so that as he was leaving for his flight to Ontario, he asked if he could call on me when I returned home. I pointed out that with him in Ontario and me in Quebec, we would be separated by more than a thousand kilometres. He smiled and said resolutely, "I will call on you." And, he did. We courted long distance from that moment in 1999 until we married a year later. The plan was that upon our marriage, I would move with him to Windsor, Ontario, to begin our new life together. Even at age thirty, I was swayed by my parents' Sicilian culture that women do not leave home until they marry.

Starting a new chapter of my life with Corrado made me feel so loved and valued. I still recall so clearly his smile and bounce as he gracefully jumped the road barrier one of the times I picked him up at the Dorval airport on his numerous visits. Or when he held me just a little bit tighter under the incredible harvest moon as we returned by motorcycle from Montebello as the chilly night air set in. From Corrado, I've learned that actions speak so much louder than words.

Words, in the form of names, and their effect on me arose as we prepared to invite guests to our wedding. Growing up, my dad was the only one to call me by a nickname, Dani. Meanwhile, family—including aunts, uncles and cousins—and family friends all called me Daniella. Almost all Italian names for girls end in *a*, so they just changed the pronunciation. I thought nothing of it until I sent out invitations for our wedding. Since Corrado and I courted long distance, he didn't get integrated into the extended family as much as most of the other fiancés. As a result, when our wedding invitations read "Danielle and Corrado," many of my cousins asked, "Who in the world are Danielle and Corrado?" How does that play on my identity?!

When Corrado and I were heading to Indonesia for our honeymoon, the question of identity arose again. We flew from Montreal to Newark to meet our connecting flight to Bali. When we went to get on the plane in Newark, we were told we could not board. Indonesia had the rule that passports had to be valid at least six months after your return date and ours were short by a few weeks. Therefore, they wouldn't let us get on the plane until we had new passports. Great, now we would get to see how the new husband and wife would handle an unexpected situation together! I am happy to report that overall, it went smoothly. We ended up staying overnight in New York City, playing tourist between running back and forth to the Canadian consulate for our passports and making phone calls to our travel agent to re-arrange our flights. We knew we would still have time to enjoy our honeymoon in Bali.

As Corrado and I were filling out the forms for the new passports, he turned to me and asked what name I intended to use. Now that we were married, he said, maybe I should take his last name. Caught up in the rush of trying to get our documents done, I agreed. I didn't even think twice about it until later when I realized that I am not Danielle Geloso. I am Danielle Saputo, aren't I? To resolve the question quickly, I hyphenated my name with his and my official documents carry that double-barreled name to this day. I'm still living the discovery that allows me to take ownership of my full self and to say that "I am enough," without shying away from the prominence that may come from the name Saputo.

The day we returned to Montreal from our honeymoon, I boxed up all my personal belongings from my parents' house and packed them into a fifteen-foot moving truck for the journey to my new home. At the age of thirty, I was happy to begin this next chapter in my life. The change did not scare me, for I knew it was going to be positive. Still, as I carried the last box out of my bedroom, I paused at the door and took one final look at the space that had been mine for the last twenty-three years, since I was seven years old. Many dreams had been dreamt in this room, and I'd had much fun within those four walls. Many late hours had been spent studying at the desk by the window that overlooked the backyard, with the beautiful view of the river. I would miss that view and this place.

Yet, I knew it was time to close the door and walk away. After all the times I'd been held back from spreading my wings, this was *my* moment. For all the times I'd been denied permission to do something I wanted to do, the day had finally come when I didn't need anyone's permission. I was a married woman now. I was with a man who I perceived would not hold me back. I had done the right thing, married a good man and made my parents proud. My reward was the freedom to go without reservation, and I embraced it with an open heart, ready and willing to make the best of whatever was to come. I was ready to start anew, to be somewhere as my true self shining bright.

Moving away from Montreal, where my name and the company Saputo Inc. were known by all, there was a relief that not everyone knew the name in my new town. I felt a weight lifted that I was not being prejudged for the name I was born with. And although this liberation gave me a sense of freedom in some ways, there were times an inner voice yelled, "I'm never good enough." One such time was when Corrado, whom I was helping with the paperwork, billings, payments and the like for his medical practice, referred to me as his secretary. "Am I just a secretary?"

this voice would say. I would be brought back to the memory at McGill University when I was told, I'm "not just a student." This insecurity did not show itself constantly, but it was within me and it was triggered occasionally. When it was triggered, it enforced the thought that I was never good enough.

I expected to suffer some homesickness when living away from my sisters and parents; the surprising truth was I didn't ... until I found out I was expecting our first child. Then I did miss them very much, especially the support they would have supplied. It was the first time I felt sadly alone, even though I felt my husband's love. It was time to plant my own seeds and grow the next branch of the family tree.

STARTING MY OWN FAMILY

Rejoice with your family in the beautiful land of life.
— Albert Einstein

I am one of those lucky women who absolutely adored being pregnant. I know not every woman feels that way because of the discomfort pregnancy brings; I was fortunate enough to feel great almost every day. I loved knowing there was a little being growing inside me. Feeling the baby move for the first time was pure joy. When she started kicking harder and flexing her tiny muscles even more, I was overcome with a sense of wonder. What a privilege and blessing it was for me to bring a new life into the world!

Enrica

The only way to live is by accepting each minute as an unrepeatable miracle.

— Tara Brach

I was at home expecting delivery of the baby's crib from Montreal on the morning my water broke. Corrado started to gather my things so we could head to the hospital. I told him I wasn't ready yet; the contractions were not sufficiently close together to warrant a dash to the maternity ward. He had planned and arranged for his sister, who lived in an apartment below us, to take me to the hospital if he wasn't home when the time came. I sent him on to work with the promise that I'd call his sister when I was ready for my ride. As soon as Corrado left, I sat down, closed my eyes, put my hands on my belly and breathed deeply. The apartment was quiet and bright; I felt very much at peace. I was mindful of the fact that I was about to enter the next stage of my life. I would no longer be simply Danielle, living for herself. I was married two years and felt the freedom of expanding my own wings: I sold quilts, I consulted entrepreneurs on business strategies, I attended the local college and took courses on photography and web page creation, I travelled to places like Japan and drove across the continent from Ontario to Arizona. I felt no limitation to my creativity and what I could do. I would now be making my way in the world as a mother, providing for and guiding a child. I felt a profound shift in my heart and soul as I contemplated this. I will always remember taking those few minutes of stillness to feel the depth of my emotions as I stepped across the threshold into motherhood. It's one of the best things I've ever done for myself.

A few hours later, our beloved Enrica was born. She was like a porcelain doll, so beautiful and perfect. The obstetrician asked Corrado if he would like to cut the umbilical cord, and he declined. I popped up and said, "I'll do it!" I was so full of energy, so taken by the beauty of bringing forth a new life. I wanted to be part of every enchanting moment.

The name Enrica is originally from the Teutonic and means "ruler of the home." Corrado and I could not have picked a more fitting title for our firstborn daughter. For all the happiness and joy she has brought me, she was also the individual who tested me in a way I'd never been tested before. Remember, I'd been alive for more than thirty years when she was born. I thought I'd seen it all. Enrica proved me wrong. She taught me that there was always something more to learn every day of my life. By the time she was five, she had pushed virtually every one of my buttons. It was still stunning to me how someone so tiny can have so much power!

Enrica put herself on a schedule from day one. She was head-strong from the start. She never fell out of the bed, never had an accident after she was out of diapers. Once her mind was made up to do something, it was done. Enrica's resourcefulness has always amazed me. When left to her own means, she was able to figure things out, be it as a toddler finding a way to get into the upper cupboard to grab her favourite snack or as a teen-ager figuring out how to get her driver's license as soon as she turned sixteen.

As challenging as she was when she was little, she was equally sweet. Every time I left or returned home, Enrica would be stand-ing at the door waving at me with a big smile. When I would head to the door to go out for groceries, she would make me stop so she could give me hug after hug after hug and a kiss and an-other hug. As I pulled the car out of the garage, she would come flying out the front door with more enthusiastic waves and a precious smile. I would drive away slowly, and she would run beside the car to the end of our property, waving until she could see me no longer. I'd watch her growing smaller in my rearview mirror, and the motherly thought crossed my mind that I should turn the car around and make her go back into the house where she'd be safe, although I knew it would be pointless. Enrica was going to do whatever she wanted. So, I'd keep driving with the faith that her guardian angel would guide her safely back into the house and keep an eye on her until I got home. (That angel worked overtime, I can assure you!)

Upon my return, Enrica would run to the garage the moment she heard me pull in, and there she would be with arms wide open to welcome me back. Although at times these displays continued many minutes after I'd said goodbye for the first time and made me late for more than one appointment, I always reminded myself that one day my daughter would probably not be so enthusiastic to see me. I'd better accept all her hugs and kisses now, while they were still being given so freely and joyously. I'm so glad I did. These gestures from Enrica were priceless—the sweetest gifts I could ever ask for.

A few months after she started high school, I arrived home around seven o'clock after a busy day running errands. I was way behind schedule. My car was full of groceries, and I still had to prepare dinner. As I came from the garage into the laundry room, lugging heavy sacks of groceries, Enrica ran up to me, put her hands out to stop me and cried, "No, Mom! Please don't come in!"

My immediate thought, feeling exhausted and rushed, was to say, "Are you kidding me?" and storm past her into the kitchen. For some reason (perhaps divine intervention), I paused instead. I happened to be studying mindfulness at the time and realized that I wanted to be alert for situations just like this one—the situations where I quickly come to my own conclusions rather than take the time to see the other person's point of view. So, instead of disregarding Enrica, I asked her how much time she needed from me.

"Maybe another seven minutes?" she said.

"Okay," I said, thinking that Enrica had stopped me for a reason. I could give her seven minutes out of my day. I called my other two daughters to take in the groceries while I stood in the laundry room waiting for who knew what.

A few minutes later, Enrica appeared at the door and said, "Okay, Mum. You can come in now." She led me into the kitchen, and there on the countertop was a dish of warm cookies that she had baked for me, alongside a thank-you card. She then proceeded to thank me for sending her to the independent school she was at. She said that she knew it was expensive, and she wanted me to know how grateful she was for the opportunity. She went on and on about it with great sincerity. I felt as if my heart would burst with love and pride.

I could have completely blown that moment, which turned out to be one of the most precious memories I have of my eldest daughter.

Olivia

> The simple things are also the most extraordinary
> things, and only the wise see them.
> — Paulo Coelho

Two years after Enrica's birth, along came Olivia. Whereas Enrica was always on an easy schedule from the beginning, Olivia gave me thirteen months of waking up every three hours. The middle of the night, first thing in the morning, late in the day, it didn't matter. Every three hours, she let me know that she needed me. I remember the beauty of going to the crib, picking her up, cuddling her, breastfeeding her and having that sweet moment of connection. Thinking back, thirteen months was a long time to go without a solid night's sleep. As time wore on and I grew more tired, I understood that as a mother I would sacrifice anything—even more than a year's worth of sound sleep—for the growth, the confidence and the security of my children. Being a mother gave me the superpower that I was capable of anything. In the process of nurturing my children I was also nurturing myself.

The name Olivia means "peacemaker," and once again Corrado and I nailed it when it came to naming a child. Our Olivia was the seeker of justice, the restorer of balance. She has an innate ability to see the not-so-obvious side of every situation. She looks deeper to see beyond what is presented to her and accepts nothing at face value. She once saw a classmate hounding another classmate and instead of instantly taking the side of the child being "picked on," she pointed out that there was probably more to the story. Maybe the "bully" was only defending himself after being mistreated by the other one, she told me. It turned out that she was correct. The ability to see the other side was one of her many gifts. Whenever something happened in front of us that appeared to be cut-and-dry, I loved to turn to Olivia and ask her how she saw it. Her eye-opening insights never failed to amaze me.

Olivia is independent. Whereas I've spent countless evenings sitting with my other two daughters helping them with their homework, I've rarely tutored Olivia. I used to feel bad about that until I realized that I haven't helped Olivia because she hasn't asked me to. Even when she was small, she managed tasks by herself. Whether it was homework or arts and crafts, she would set up her workspace with all her crayons lined up in colour order and her other supplies in place. She was very particular about this; if I tried to enter the area and influence her actions in any way, she would ask me to stop. She did things in her space and her way.

As a parent, I learned to respect my children and give them the space they need. I had to remind myself that their need of me was different, and each child didn't need my presence equally.

Eventually, I figured out that when Olivia wanted my help, she would let me know.

Aurelia

> The smallest act of kindness is worth more than the greatest intention.
>
> *— Kahlil Gibran*

Last and certainly not least came Aurelia. Her birth has been forever seared into my psyche because I knew she would be my final child. I recognized that after carrying, birthing and nursing three children, my body had given all that it could give. At thirty-six I would bear no more children; I felt the depletion childbirth had on the body. It was a bittersweet realization. All three of my girls are kind and considerate people, yet Aurelia takes kindness and consideration a step further. Her name comes from the Latin for "golden," and she is indeed a golden treasure. Ultrasensitive, empathetic and aware, she'd usually be the first to inquire if everything was okay.

Whereas Enrica had me sleeping a solid night by three months and Olivia kept me awake for more than a year, Aurelia was intermittent. There was no fixed schedule with her. The worst was when I would be awakened after hearing a hard *thud* in her room. I would run in to find that Aurelia had fallen out of her bed, again. Sometimes she would still be asleep on the floor; other times I'd find her awake, startled and unsure of what had just happened. I would tuck her back in, and she would go right back to sleep.

Back when there were only my first two children, Enrica and Olivia, in the house, the world revolved around their sleeping and feeding schedules. By the time Aurelia was born, her sisters were involved in many activities: playgroups, music, dance, library time, swimming lessons and art at the community centre. We were on the go constantly, so she was forced to be flexible. It didn't matter whether she was asleep or hungry, she had to get in the car and go... now! Did I feel guilty about that sometimes? Of course. Thinking back, would I change anything? Not really. The guilt came because at this stage of my life, my focus was on being the best parent I could be, loving and nurturing each of my children, exposing them to experiences that would keep them well-rounded, active participants in their community. Interrupting my newborn's sleep to keep a schedule I set did have some guilt attached. There was always the question, even though it had no words at the time—am I enough?

When Aurelia was seven years old, she joined the Girl Guides and was at the age of being a Brownie. Her first overnight trip was approaching, and she was very excited ... that is, until she found out that the trip was scheduled on my birthday weekend. She was in a dilemma because she really wanted to go and she really wanted to be with me on my birthday too. I asked her if she'd like for me to go on the trip as a volunteer so that she could have both the trip and me. "Yes! That would be wonderful!" was the happy reply.

I ended up accompanying her for the trip, and we had a beautiful time. This worked out great all the way around, because Enrica and Olivia were also in Guides and doing an overnight campout at the same place. On my birthday, I was together with my three favourite girls. The outing itself was lovely, thanks to my golden girl Aurelia, the master of the unexpected, and upon arrival at the camp as I was making up our beds, I found a little gift and a card that she had hidden away in her bag to give to me later. She had prepared them all by herself as a birthday surprise for me. Such a sweet delight! That's Aurelia in a nutshell.

Each of my daughters shared her own gifts with me, based on her unique personality. I thought that as a mother I would treat all my children the same, and once I had three, I knew that was an impossible dream. Birth order matters. In *The Birth Order Book: Why You Are The Way You Are*, psychologist Dr. Kevin Leman[6] states that first-time parents will often turn into by-the-book caregivers who focus on every detail and set firm rules for the first born child and anyone caring for him or her. The child becomes the centre of attention without competition from other siblings. As a result, they get more time and more complete explanations to their questions. As the leader of the pack, firstborns often tend to be reliable, conscientious, structured, cautious, controlling and achievers.

When a second child comes along, most parents lighten up as they feel more confident and comfortable in their roles. They are less attentive to every detail of the second baby as they also raise another child, who is likely a busy and mobile toddler. They are more open to giving a second child the freedom to sleep at a friend's house sooner than they did with their firstborn. Middle children tend to possess the following personality traits: people-pleasing, somewhat rebellious, thriving on friendships, having a large social circle and peacemaking.

Parental attention becomes even more relaxed and divided when a third baby arrives. The youngest children are allowed more leeway in rules and in household duties, yet often have their achievements compared to those of their older siblings. The baby of the family tends to have the following traits: fun-loving, uncomplicated, manipulative, outgoing, attention-seeking and self-centred.

As parents focus on setting new rules for each new phase for the older child, while supervising the needs of the youngest, the middle child can get lost in between. In fact, a survey by TheBabyWebsite.com, a British parenting resource, revealed that 33 percent of parents with three children confess that they paid far less attention to their middle child than their other offspring.[7] I can relate as I tried to juggle the needs and personalities of our three girls.

After Aurelia was born, I had an experience I will never forget because it was one of those horrible moments when I had to choose between my girls. I was taking the three of them for a walk. Aurelia, who was only a few weeks old, was in her stroller. Enrica, four, and Olivia, two, were holding on to the stroller, one on each side, when suddenly they took off in a beeline in opposite directions. I was like a deer caught in the headlights for a moment. *Oh my God, do I leave this tiny baby alone in the stroller and give chase? And if I do give chase, which one should I go after first? Olivia is only two and Enrica moves faster.* I remember going through that thought process in a nanosecond.

In the end, what did I actually do? I don't remember. I must have blocked it out. I just remember suddenly having them all herded back together without recalling the steps I took to get there. The hard lesson was that I couldn't protect all three of them all the time. This was a stark realization for me, as up to that point, being a parent, I believed my superpower was the ability to do it all.

Looking back, I don't know how my mother did it all with five children. We did ballet and swimming. We played soccer. We figure skated. We were in school plays. Some of us did horseback riding, judo and skiing. She had all of us playing instruments, mainly piano. Meanwhile, I had my hands full taking care of *three* little girls. Just like my mother, there were moments when I blew up on days when my patience was truly short. Sometimes I was proud of how I managed these moments, and other times I wish I had responded with more composure.

On one such occasion, Enrica entered my room and began playing with my backup pair of eyeglasses. When I walked in, I saw her looking as if I'd caught her with her hand in the cookie jar. Then I saw the cupboard and box of my personal belongings opened, my bent eyeglasses perched on her forehead and more of my things strewn about. I did not hold back. My voice bellowed out before I had the chance to think it through.

"How dare you!" I yelled. "Never touch Mummy's things without asking!"

This was the first time I'd raised my voice so loudly that I scared my little girl. The words themselves were not terrible—the tone was. I could have been yelling "I love you!" except the manner in which I spoke said only one thing to my daughter: *"You did something wrong!"* Worst of all, she didn't understand what she had done to warrant such a response from me. How could she? She was only playing with a pile of interesting things. She plays with interesting things all the time. Why would this time merit such a response?

Without an explanation, there was only contradiction, confusion and a door open to interpretation about why it's okay to play with some things and not others. She needed clarification, and I was too furious to provide it—furious mostly at myself. My choice of how to respond was harsh and hasty, especially for someone who had stark memories of facing my parents' wrath while growing up. As I looked at Enrica's shocked little face, I was ashamed of myself. I've often wondered if my mother felt the same shame after she slapped me for greeting the boy with a kiss on the cheek one afternoon without explaining to me why it was wrong. I imagine she did. Forgiving her for that omission is a lot easier now that I've walked a mile in her shoes as a mother. I sat Enrica on my lap, held her close and explained myself. I used these words: I'm sorry, please forgive me, thank you, I love you. Years later, I learned this is a beautiful Hawaiian teaching about forgiveness called Ho'oponopono (making it right).

There were also the good days, such as when I found Enrica and Olivia playing with the little bit of makeup I owned. Although I thought I had this bag of cosmetics completely out of reach, resourceful Enrica again proved me wrong. I found her applying lipstick to Olivia's face, completely missing her lips, by the way. They were both painted up and believed they looked gorgeous. This time I had my wits with me. I left the room, collected my camera and filmed them together as two tiny sisters completely enjoying each other's company. As I did so, I made a wish that they would be like this with each other forever—together in this harmony and music of delight, two little girls who were in bliss, and me, finding joy in this scene if I looked past the fact that they were using my treasured makeup. Enrica had entered a space she was not supposed to be in, and now I had another cleanup job to add to my long list of things to do. The choice of how to respond was still mine, though. Did I focus on the upside or the downside of this wacky scene in front of me? That day I chose the upside. I managed to speak calmly as I told them to please not touch what the girls called Mummy's "colours" ever again.

The summer when my girls were one, three and five, we were having some landscaping done to a home we had just moved into. The landscapers needed some questions answered, so I left my girls in the playroom while I stepped out into the backyard. Upon my return just a few moments later, I found all three of them playing innocently on what they believed was a big pile of white sand. Aurelia, who was barely walking at the time, was dipping her index finger into the white granular substance and putting it in her mouth. I stared in disbelief as her finger went from her mouth to white substance to mouth again. Then I saw the upside-down (now empty) box of laundry detergent sitting off to the side of the pile. The panic that came chilled my blood.

I quickly herded my little ones away from the white powder and called poison control. There was no benefit to throwing blame towards anyone. My focus here was to find a solution and confirm that everyone was okay. This time it was Enrica who'd had the ingenious idea to try to entertain her sisters in my absence. In addition to observing my own reaction, which I handled with enough calm, I learned to put out of reach any toxic household products and to teach the girls that they were not to play with items that have danger symbols on them. Luckily, none of them were poisoned!

If I were asked what lessons I've learned through these stories I shared, I would say, "Watch how you make assumptions about your children." Although Enrica did have a track record of being the one to cause mischief, she wasn't the only culprit. Once, I was at a mall kiosk, settling a problem with my cell phone provider.

Aurelia was in the stroller in front of me, and my back was to
the other two. I turned around a moment into my conversation
with the representative to find Enrica and Olivia gone. Ten long
minutes later, I found them on the floor "swimming" on top of
dozens upon dozens of glossy brochures and pamphlets that
Olivia had pulled down from the mall information display racks.

I took just a moment to be mindful and compose myself, for they
did look quite cute sprawled out on the floor. I could not laugh
with them. If I did, I would not be able to teach them an important lesson. I could not yell at them either since I didn't want
to teach them to respond to life's surprises with anger. Every
occurrence like this represents a teaching moment, so as some
skilled mothers learn to do, I managed to smile and frown at the
same time. I asked my two little "swimmers" if they were done.
Then, with great restraint and all the gentleness I could muster,
I said, "These brochures do not belong on the floor. Someone
took a lot of time and care to place them on the racks so others
could use them to find their way around the mall. Would you be
so kind as to put them back where they belong?"

With wide smiles, they quickly began picking them up and returning them to the racks. Several passersby were kind enough
to stop and help, too. I marveled at the benevolence of those
strangers. They had stopped to help me, not knowing the family
I was from or my last name. They helped simply because they
saw that I needed it. My trust in people grew a little bit that day.
Together we turned chaos back into order, and I continued on
with my errands.

> *Raise your words, not voice. It is rain*
> *that grows flowers, not thunder.*
>
> *—Rumi*

Parenting, like many other roles in life, is a beautiful thing. I've learned to be mindful, to not view surprises like the laundry detergent and brochures as problems, rather as gifts that life presents to me as opportunities to grow and teach my girls. One of my favourite examples of mindfulness (and respect) comes from parking the children in front of the television to remain safely occupied while we prepared dinner or did some other essential chore. It's okay; we all do it from time to time! When I do, it's important to consider their feelings before calling them to dinner. If I expected them to jump and run to the table as soon as they were called before the episode of their favourite show was over, I was asking too much. Nobody likes to be interrupted while enjoying a fun activity. Be mindful. Take note of when their program will be finished and give them a five-minute warning before the show ends. These little acts of mindful moments, of being considerate and respectful of their feelings, create a stronger parent/child relationship and bond. Being aware and having this level of mindfulness was a leap forward to stepping into the sunlight of my true self.

Children are so attuned to the subtle cues that we send them. These cues shape their behaviour, and they don't realize that they are adapting. Just like the silent clues I received as a child, my girls often read more than intended into the messages they received from the adults in their lives.

My goal in parenting was to be present around the school, so my children saw how much I valued their education. Back when my daughter Olivia was in junior kindergarten class, I offered to help out in the classroom. The teacher thanked me and declined, explaining that young children tended not to react well when a parent was present in the classroom. I didn't persist and respected the teacher to know what was best in her classroom.

Flash forward a couple of years to when my youngest, Aurelia, started junior kindergarten. I like to think that my continual presence of walking my children to and from school every day with our West Highland White Terrier Jojo in tow spoke volumes about the person I was: always present, kind and together with my girls. Apparently, Ms. Tucker, the kindergarten teacher, recognized that because when I volunteered to help out again, she accepted my offer. Aurelia was standing beside me that day, and the teacher turned to her and said, "Your mom can help out, but when she's in the room, you can't let anyone know that she's your mother. Understood?" Aurelia nodded resolutely since she tried to do the right and considerate thing. She then went off to play with her new friends. All was well, right?

Maybe not. When an authority figure tells a four-year-old—especially an ultraconscientious four-year-old like Aurelia—something important like that, get ready for some major compliance. For years after the comment her kindergarten teacher made, whenever Aurelia and I were around the school (or even around her friends off campus) and I would try to give her a hug and a kiss, she would stiffen up like a little tin soldier. She was determined not to let anybody know that I was her mother. When we were at home, however, she was stuck to me like glue. This goes to show the power of words, especially in the hearts and minds of our younger ones.

Structural Stability or Shaky Ground?

> *In an age of constant acceleration, nothing can*
> *be more exhilarating than going slow. In an age*
> *of constant distraction, nothing is so luxurious*
> *as paying attention. In an age of constant*
> *movement, nothing is so urgent as sitting still.*
>
> — Pico Iyer

If you've ever grown a bonsai tree, you know that it's a painstaking process and an object lesson in patience. Slow, constant care and skillful pruning; that's what little bonsais need if they are to grow in the best way possible. My girls have taught me that motherhood is similar to being a bonsai grower. I don't know when (or if) that sense of being a mother hen will ever diminish. After nineteen years, it hasn't happened yet.

As I write this, I reflect on when Enrica came back from a three-month grade ten student exchange in Australia. Such a trip was not easy for an introvert like Enrica. Upon her return, she told me, "There's beauty in opening myself up. The friendships and the memories I made in Australia are phenomenal." When she came to me saying that she wanted to go to Australia at age sixteen, my immediate thought was to say, "No, that is too far from home for such a young lady." Thankfully, I resisted that urge. Instead, Enrica and I sat down and had an open conversation about it. After listening to her explain her rationale for wanting to go to that particular place so far away, I gave her my blessing. It turns out it was the right thing to do. The trip was an incredible growing experience for her.

I am determined to give my girls more opportunities like that exchange trip. When I was seventeen, I had the chance to travel to Neuchâtel, Switzerland, for a year of schooling, and my parents declined to let me go. I've always wondered what gifts I might have found there, what transitions of my own I might have experienced. As a result, my mindset in raising my daughters is that life is short. The world is our playground; there's so much to see and learn out there. We grow when we go. I had imagined that I could take a step back once they became independent, and as they have become teenagers, there have been many sure signs of independence. When I mentioned that to our pediatrician, he smiled and shook his head.

"They will need your consistent guidance until they're at least twenty-four," he said. "So, settle in, Mom. You have a long way to go."

That was fine with me. I love being a mother. I love teaching my girls the value of stewardship and the power of connection and family. For all the things I've taught my girls, they've taught me even more. They—along with my grandparents, parents, sisters and husband—are my foundation. They make me want to be my highest self every single day.

I believe that my girls are good enough and smart enough to choose their own way. They are not just "my daughters." They are individual human beings with ideas and needs and wishes separate from mine. In reflecting on my daughters and everything they have taught me, I am reminded of this glorious passage from Kahlil Gibran's *The Prophet*:[8]

Your children are not your children.
They are the sons and daughters of Life's longing for itself.
They come through you but not from you,
And though they are with you yet they belong not to you.

You may give them your love but not your thoughts,
For they have their own thoughts.

You may house their bodies but not their souls,
For their souls dwell in the house of tomorrow, which
you cannot visit, not even in your dreams.
You may strive to be like them, but seek
not to make them like you.
For life goes not backward nor tarries with yesterday.
You are the bows from which your children
as living arrows are sent forth.
The archer sees the mark upon the path of the infinite, and He
bends you with His might that His arrows may go swift and far.
Let your bending in the archer's hand be for gladness;
For even as He loves the arrow that flies, so
He loves also the bow that is stable.

Every parent would do well to read these wise words at least once a month!

Although I have learned many lessons and felt satisfied with many aspects of my life, an increasing pang of insignificance brewed. Even a mighty oak with a strong foundation can have weak points and crack under stress and strain. Like so many women, I often felt "less than" in many aspects of my life. I questioned my parenting skills and whether I was doing the best I could do for my three girls. I had no title when asked, "What do you do?" My husband called me a secretary, and my sister referred to me as a housewife, which toyed with my ego and had me ask, "Am I just that?" All my accomplishments to date felt insignificant. I wasn't on a typical career path working for the family business or another firm. I had lived away from my childhood home for over fifteen years and was beginning to feel a sense of disconnection. I was terribly confused and conflicted by that feeling, and it only increased around the time I was in my midforties. How could I be surrounded by this much abundance, love and goodness and still feel so alone and insignificant sometimes? It was then that I began taking a hard look at myself and began putting into practice the many learnings I had gathered.

In the pages that follow, I will share with you these learnings, which are tools I've gathered throughout my journey. The tools I will be sharing with you helped me be my own guru to self-discovery, allowing me to step into the sunlight of my true self. My aim is not to come across as a self-help expert. My intention is that by sharing, you will find something that works for you and that you too will have confirmation that I, you, we are enough.

THE LANGUAGE I USE AND THE NEED TO CELEBRATE

The more you celebrate your life, the
more there is in life to celebrate.
— Oprah Winfrey

In the summer of 2010, now settled in Peterborough, my girls and I had our first experience participating in a triathlon, a sport in which competitors swim, bike and run for several kilometres without a break. I completed my first attempt at a full tri, and my girls experienced Dr. Katy Shufelt's Kids Triathlon, which was described by the organizers as an event to "encourage kids to be active and healthy while introducing them to the joy of triathlon." My daughters were four, six and eight at the time. The highlight of the day was seeing my girls receiving their medals and standing on the podium with a great sense of accomplishment.

When I was growing up, our family celebrated important holidays and personal milestones like birth and death, birthdays, weddings, graduations, religious holidays and company anniversaries. Individual accomplishments were not acknowledged in the same way, and after each of my accomplishments, I'd often think, So that's done; so what's the next task?

I wanted so much more for my girls. I will never forget the proud grins on their faces, the way they carried themselves with such satisfaction after the completion of their triathlon. Each participant received a medal as they passed the finish line, a token to remind each athlete of a job well done. I took it a step further and had them pose on the podium set up by the organization. I took photos, they posed and showed off their medals, we danced and we made it a celebratory awards ceremony. They felt like rock stars and couldn't wait to show their medals to their dad and the loved ones around them. Afterwards, they hung their medals where they could see them every day. Looking at their prize and remembering their achievements gave them a boost of confidence and the desire to get back out there and try again.

That's the power of celebration.

When I was about to turn forty, I had birthed three children and felt not-so-fit, more than a little sluggish and clumsy, the opposite of energetic and flexible. I wanted to get back into shape, so I joined a gym. It was there that I met some people who participate in triathlons. Training for one appealed to my adventurous nature and, of course, to my quest to become stronger. Triathletes are the very definition of strength. I decided to join their ranks and give the sport a try.

My original idea was to work up to it gradually and be ready for my first race in five years, yet multiple trainers told me I was capable of participating in the coming season. I spent the winter in the pool, in spin classes and on the treadmill. It felt great to have a positive new challenge to look forward to. My training was sporadic, having three young girls at home; however, I was determined to keep it up. I even trained while on a trip to Las Vegas with my female cousins in July 2010, after I was officially registered for the Chemong Lake Tri. Running in Las Vegas was memorable. The heat, the landscape and the early-morning desert sun were a big change from what I was used to back in Ontario. After running in Las Vegas each day, I would jump into the hotel pool and do laps until I was out of breath. I couldn't wait to compete in my first competition.

Race day came and although I hadn't simulated a full race prior to the event, I knew I could do each of the legs easily on their own: a 300-metre swim, a 10K bike ride and a 3K run. I'd never practiced a transition (going from swimming to bicycling or bicycling to running), nor had I done an open water swim before. Still, I was confident. I left the house alone early that morning with great excitement. I'd skydived, bungee-jumped, white water rafted, swam with dolphins in the Indian Ocean, rode a camel in the African Sahara and learned to handle a motorcycle. Now I was ready to accomplish yet another challenge, the most grueling one to date.

The race began with the swim segment. I'm a slow and steady swimmer and had been advised by veteran triathletes not to get caught at the front of the crowd at takeoff, so I fell back and began my swim behind the others. As I made my way through the course, my front crawl turned to a breaststroke that turned to a sidestroke that turned to backstroke and finally became strokes that I made up as I went along. Open water swimming in Chemong Lake was much different from doing laps in a pool. I admit that I was a bit discouraged. As I came around the second turn to head back towards land, I raised my head to take a breath and caught sight of an older gentleman swimming in front of me. I came up again and realized that he wasn't just swimming in front of me, he was swimming towards me. I began to question if I was going the right way.

I continued my stroke and kept my head above water, trying to comprehend what was going on. My fatigued brain battled with itself: the land is that way, I'm sure of it ... at least, I think it's that way ... then why is he swimming towards me? ... Oh, I'm so confused! In my determination to keep going, I finally realized what was happening. The man was caught in a current. He was not moving forward at all; the current was too strong. As I passed him, I marveled at the power of perspective and how different things look when my mind was set on one thought. At last, I made it to shore, with seaweed dangling from my limbs. I collected my glasses from the kind spectator, a stranger in the crowd who'd held on to them for me (another reinforcement that there are good people in this world who do good just to do good, not because they wanted something in return from me as a Saputo). From there, I continued on to complete the biking and running segments. My first triathlon was a wonderful experience and a great accomplishment, as well as a real-world lesson on perspective.

In 2012, we repeated the experience. Aurelia was still using training wheels and smiled right through to the finish line after completing a 50-metre swim, a 1K bike ride and a 500-metre run. Olivia had a similar experience and was completely parched after a 50-metre swim, a 3.8K bike ride and a 1K run. She made it through the finish line, standing and smiling. Enrica, who was put into the highest category as a ten-year-old, completed a 100-metre swim, a 5.7K bike ride and a 1.5K run. The pride I felt as she crossed that finish line was immense. Enrica, on the other hand, did not share my pride. She felt completely defeated, saying, "But I came in last!" Although she was not the last to cross the finish line, she had seen many people passing her on the run (which, by the way, she had not trained for) and every aspect of her body language spoke defeat. I thought, Enrica, are you kidding me? You swam, biked and ran eight kilometres without stopping, "but" you didn't finish first? The word "but" minimized Enrica's achievement, affecting her attitude and ours as well.

"But" I've done better in the past. "But" so-and-so beat me. "But" I could have also done X, Y, Z. What an unfortunate, negative, judgmental word "but" is. It is a thief that robs us of so many good feelings. Rather than saying "but," what if we practiced saying "yes, *and*" instead? Imagine if Enrica had crossed the finish line saying, "Yes, I entered the race *and* I finished it! And I can't wait to do it again next year!" What a difference! All of us would have felt our spirits rise as we envisioned her running and finishing next year's race. It's just a great example of the power of our language to either drain us or energize us. As the inspirational Tony Robbins[9] writes in his book *Awaken the Giant Within: How to Take Immediate Control of Your Mental, Emotional, Physical and Financial Destiny!*, it's all about "the state" we put ourselves in.

In every moment, I can reframe my experience with the words I choose to perceive and describe it. If I focus on the negative points in my day, they will dominate my thoughts and my words. And, if I diminish or neutralize their importance and let the good moments shine through, I will become more resilient and content with my accomplishments. What I tell others also confirms how I feel about what has happened or will happen. Don't hold back on positive thoughts and words. The language I use talking to myself and speaking to others has great power.

Finishing a triathlon was no small task and definitely needs to be celebrated!

My next event, the Stony Lake Tri, also took place in 2012, and it was a different experience. I arrived for the start of the race to find all the other competitors in wet suits. I'd brought mine with no intention to use it because I had not worn it during my practice swims. In preparation, several competitors convinced me that the buoyancy the suit gives would be to my advantage and would keep me warmer (the water temperature was estimated to be a chilly seventy degrees Fahrenheit that early June day). I decided to go along with the crowd and wear my wet suit, against my better judgment.

The start of the race was stalled and confusing. Initially, we were told to be at the marina's boat ramp to begin our swim, then suddenly we were moved to the boat docks and then abruptly moved again to a new start line. All this last-minute shuffling had placed me in the middle of the pack, disrupting my strategy of starting at the rear. Suddenly the horn blew.

The race was on. I moved forward with the crowd.

My mind was not in champion mode at this point. As I began the swim with a front crawl, I struggled to regain my positive attitude in the midst of the frantic kicking and splashing from all the bodies around me. I tried to reassure myself with an internal pep talk: Danielle, you're doing great … you're so strong … stroke, stroke, stroke … relax! Just as I was getting into my groove, something struck the top of my head so hard that I went under. It felt like someone had hit me with a club. I missed a breath, inhaled water and stalled. The culprit was another swimmer who was too close to me. As she reached forward with her front crawl stroke, the full force of her upper arm hit me squarely on the head. I was disoriented and coughing as I struggled to move forward. I tried to catch my breath, to relax all the muscles in my body, to *breathe* and I could not. The wet suit was constricting; it felt too tight. I needed air. My only thought was to get out of that wet suit *now*. The signal for help was to wave your bathing cap, so that's what I did. A race assistant paddled towards me quickly in his kayak.

"What do you need?" he asked.

"Need … to … take … the … suit … off!" I panted.

I reached for my back zipper cord and couldn't catch hold of it. I heard the assistant yell out to another race official, "Can they take off their wet suit?" I grabbed the kayak and shook it to get his attention. I looked him squarely in the eye.

"I have to take it off!" I said decisively.

At that moment, he realized that I no longer cared about the rules of the contest. For a woman who grew up following the rules and being compliant, it was a huge step to express myself so clearly. That suit was coming off. I don't know how we managed to remove a skintight wet suit in the water. Ultimately, it was clear, with determination, I can achieve impossible things. After a lot of pulling and tugging, it came off and I was free. My chest expanded and I could *breathe*. I gave my kind helper a thumbs-up and continued on my way to completing another triathlon. Determination always wins the day. In the heat of the race, I've learned to tell myself that I want to see what happens when I don't give up!

The last event I entered was not the typical individual race. This team sprint triathlon had squads of three athletes competing against other squads. Each athlete performs one leg of the race, which consists of a 750-metre swim, a 20K bike ride and a 5K run. I entered the competition with the idea that I was going to do the bike portion, for which I was more than ready. I had been biking since the spring and was easily putting in 40K twice a week. To my surprise, I was assigned the run portion. A neighbourly friend was forming teams for this event, and I did say I would be happy to enter and be part of a squad. I did not specify I wanted to do the bike portion. I did have the expectation that since we biked together, she was aware that that was my preferred sport. A lesson to self: without communicating, expectations can lead to disappointments. I had not done any running for some time and had considered it my weak sport; my body was simply not made for running. Having said that, I was excited to be part of the team. The 5K was a short run and I knew I could do it, although perhaps not as fast as the others.

The day of the event turned out to be excruciatingly hot. There was no respite from the beating sun, and I felt the heat of the asphalt penetrating the soles of my running shoes. My breathing was laboured. Those five kilometres seemed as if they would never end. On the last stretch—which culminated with a sharp uphill run—I mustered my last ounce of energy to make it through the finish line with a cheer. My teammates were there alongside others who had gathered together for the event. That sense of being on a team, of being part of something greater than myself, was supremely satisfying. Another day worth living! It brought me a deep sense of purpose and fulfillment and taught me that it's not about making the top ten. It's about being my best every day. It makes the impossible possible.

Having my friends boost my spirits with their cheers meant so much to me that day. Their actions reinforced for me the idea that celebrations need not be elaborate or expensive to be effective. They didn't shower me with champagne or hand me a bouquet of roses. Their presence and their sincere voices were all I needed to feel as though I was enough—and more than I ever expected to be as an athlete. Celebrations only have to be positive, mindful commemorations of having taken a step forward. Have you ever seen one of those signs in a manufacturing plant or other facility that reads, "'X' Days Without a Workplace Accident! Thank You for Working Safely!" That's an example of a simple, inexpensive acknowledgement of a positive action that deserves celebration. When my child brought home a math worksheet to which the teacher had affixed a shiny gold star, this was another modest reward for a tiny yet noteworthy achievement. Even a humble reward like a gold star or a thumbs-up poster can be a great motivator. My girls and I have a high five or "celebration dance" when we acknowledge something noteworthy.

Here are some other modest ways to celebrate:

- Treat yourself to something special: a nice bottle of wine, lunch or dinner at your favourite restaurant, a new outfit, a flower bouquet, a trip to a day spa, a day out to watch your favourite sports team. The "something special" doesn't have to be elaborate or expensive. It only has to signal "celebration" and help you acknowledge your small step forward.

- Take a walk, all by yourself, with the sole purpose of reflecting on your progress. Whether it's a hike through the woods or a walk along the beach or a simple stroll around your neighbourhood, be mindful of your feet taking literal steps forward. In your mind, link those steps with the other kinds of steps you are taking in your personal growth. Breathe in the fresh air deeply. Feel the sunlight (or the moonlight) caressing your skin. Hear the wind rustling through the trees, the waves crashing on the shore.

Stop for a moment and allow yourself to feel gratitude for how far you've come and for the gift of being alive.

- Spend an hour making a collage or other art piece that expresses your feelings about your latest small win. Hang it where you can see it every day.
- Take a mental photograph. Close your eyes, visualize the moment, sear it in your memory, take a slow breath in—hold—out, open your eyes and the mental photograph is taken.
- Create a handwritten thank-you note to someone who has helped you in your journey. Expressing your appreciation for others is a form of celebration.

You get the idea. There are countless ways to acknowledge my efforts. Even the smallest reward can be enough to help me stay on track and reinvigorate me. I keep in mind to involve my loved ones in my celebrations as well, especially my children. I let them see me striving to reach for my highest self. I let them see my gratitude for life—including my gratitude for setbacks and challenges, for they represent rich opportunities for learning and growth, too. By inviting my children into these moments of acknowledgement and commemoration, I teach them how to cultivate a grateful and celebratory spirit. What a lovely gift I give them. Just the thought of it makes me want to go out and celebrate!

Of course, the journey begins with me committing to taking on an activity that can make me feel like a winner. How I get to that stage requires some key questions—more than I expected—and digging deeper into what motivates me and drives me forward. It's all about knowing my *Why?*

GETTING TO THE BOTTOM LINE

Knowing yourself is the beginning of all wisdom.
—*Aristotle*

When I was looking for a way to get back into shape and started telling family and friends that I was considering becoming a triathlete, I received a mixed reaction. Most people thought it sounded like a great idea; a few told me I was nuts. Regardless of their opinions, everyone agreed that I had a huge challenge ahead of me. Honestly, I wasn't sure I had what it takes to be a triathlete. I began asking elite athletes for words of wisdom and their best tips and tricks. One of them (I'll call him David) gave me some advice I've carried with me and used in virtually every aspect of my life since: If I want to succeed at a big challenge I have to tap into the power of *why*. I can't settle for the first reason that pops into my head. Take my triathlon dream as an example. When David asked me why I wanted to pursue the sport, I replied that I wanted to get in shape. He shook his head.

"No, that's not enough," he said. "I'm not talking about something as obvious as 'get in shape.' I'm talking about the profound reasons; the deep, intimate soul-level reasons why you say you want to achieve this goal. If you don't know those deep reasons, Danielle, you're not going to be able to withstand the pressure and pain of this sport."

At that, David challenged me to write a list of the 25 Reasons Why I wanted to be a triathlete. He told me that the exercise sounds a lot easier than it is, and that's why it's so powerful. Having to think of so many reasons for wanting to do something forced me to drill down past the superficial shallows and into the depths where my true self resided. Once I'd established that conduit to my most genuine self, I became "powerful beyond measure," as described by author Marianne Willamson.[10]

I couldn't wait to get home and write out my 25 Reasons Why. The first few reasons came to me easily:

1. Get in shape.
2. Stay in shape.
3. Have something positive/constructive to do every day.
4. Meet inspiring people.
5. Spend more time outdoors.
6. Do something just for me.
7. Participate in cool events.

After that, the *whys* were harder to come by. I doubted I'd ever make it to twenty-five, although at this point I put my trust in David's advice and kept going. The trick here is to keep pen to paper and keep writing. There is power in getting out of the headspace and into the heart space. What a rewarding journey and what a difficult struggle! By the time I got down to the last few reasons, I was overcome with emotion and surprised by what

I'd learned about myself. It turns out that my triathlon dream had surprisingly little to do with physical fitness and everything to do with conquering my feelings of inadequacy. It was about proving to the family patriarch and matriarch (and, of course, myself) that I am capable of great things. It was about showing my daughters that we are all "powerful beyond measure" and that the purpose of life is to *live*.

With all of that as my motivation, I knew I could move mountains. On the many occasions when I felt that I couldn't go on during a race—such as when the other participant struck my head during the swim or when my feet felt as if they were on fire while running—I've summoned my top reasons why and gained an instant jolt of strength and resolve. I use this exercise whenever I set a big audacious goal (like writing this book!), and it helps me overcome every obstacle I encounter on the way to making my dreams come true.

What's Important Now?

> *Right now is the Best Time to create your Tomorrow.*
> — Ken Poirot

I love listening to motivational speakers for inspiration. A few of my favourites are Brené Brown, Byron Katie, the Dalai Lama, Siri Lindley, Simon Sinek, Tony Robbins and Marianne Williamson. I came across another one recently—American football coach turned motivational speaker Lou Holtz—who surprised me with his simple yet powerful insight. Holtz was one of the most successful coaches in the history of US college football and has inspired countless young athletes since launching his career in the late 1960s. His message centres on the notion that to achieve greatness, I need look no further than the present moment because that is where I'll find my ultimate power. To remind his players of this truth, Holtz created a simple question that he calls WIN: What's Important Now?

The great coach understood that we achieve our goals one step and one choice at a time. So, he instructed his student athletes to ask themselves, "What's Important Now?" at least thirty-five times a day. In other words, "What can I do right now, in this moment, to take myself one step closer to being a champion?" For Holtz's players, the answer first thing in the morning would probably be, "Eat a nourishing breakfast." A few minutes later, the answer might be, "Study my playbook." After that, "Hit the gym and do my toughest workout." Later, "Pay attention in class so I can get good grades and keep my scholarship." Later still, "Take the time to lace up my cleats properly so I don't get blisters on my feet." This continues throughout the day, until the young man's entire day has been spent taking one small yet important step after another towards greatness. How simple and elegant is that?

Asking myself, "What's Important Now?" kept me grounded in the present moment and helped me avoid rehashing past mistakes or worrying about a future I can't control. It also helped me prioritize tasks when I had a million things on my plate and kept me from getting bogged down in "wishful thinking mode." Have you ever wanted something very badly—say, to lose weight, or take up painting or writing, or buy a new house, or exit an unhealthy relationship—yet you could never get beyond the point of dreaming about it? It's nice to have those kinds of visions for the future. After all, lying awake at night fantasizing about being a waist size smaller than I am or winning the Nobel Prize in Literature is fruitless because I'm focusing my attention on an outcome, not on how to get it.

Answering Holtz's WIN question kept my focus and concentration on the action steps I can take right now, in the present moment ... which is really the only thing I can control. Those actions are what made the difference, going beyond using my will to change my current situation.

When I was trying to do something challenging like run a triathlon—or live a fulfilling life—I increased my odds of success when I knew myself: my personal strengths, values, passions and fears; my intimate reasons for doing what I do; and my action steps for achieving my goals. The knowledge of who I am, what I'm trying to do with my life and what I stand for (and what I won't stand for) helped me over the hump during those exhausting and confusing moments I had to face. I drew on them when things weren't going the way I hoped or when I didn't know which way to turn. How did I gain this self-knowledge? By asking myself for the answers, of course! I know that "asking myself for answers" may sound super simple. Let me ask you this: If it's so simple, why don't more of us do it? I think the answer is that we don't know how or what to ask.

Bottom-Line Questions

> *Quality questions create a quality life.*
> *Successful people ask better questions, and*
> *as a result, they get better answers.*
>
> — *Tony Robbins*

That brings me to my Bottom-Line Questions. I refer to them as the "bottom line" for two reasons. First, I come from a business family. I majored in business in university, and I manage my immediate family's wealth today. In business and personal finance, I make decisions based upon what I imagine the impact will be on my net profit as represented by the number on the literal bottom line of a financial report. I'm accustomed to thinking of things that way. The second reason is a bit warmer and fuzzier. The term "bottom line" also means the crux of the matter. The most essential point. The primary consideration. Recalling and answering my Bottom-Line Questions reminds me instantly of what's most important to me. They snap me back into alignment whenever I'm feeling weak, scattered, confused or out of balance.

I believe that asking myself the WIN question multiple times every day and challenging myself to come up with 25 Reasons Why are quality questions. And I've come up with a few additional Bottom-Line Questions that I like to ask myself and my clients from time to time, especially in those moments when I feel unsteady or confused about the right path forward.

Some bottom-line questions are as follows:

- What are my core values? (Core values are fundamental beliefs and guiding principles.)
- What are my greatest passions, and what is stopping me from pursuing them? (Passions include activities I feel driven to learn more about and tasks that make me want to go the extra mile without having to be asked.)
- What am I afraid of? (This could be basic human fears like injustice, physical pain, death, rejection, failure and surprisingly, success.) Coming from an entrepreneurial family, I fear success because I know how much hard work goes into achieving it and how much intense pressure there is in maintaining it.
- What are my strengths? (Strengths include activities I do well, my talents, skills and knowledge.)

The lovely thing about these questions is that I can use them to reframe the experiences of daily life in a way that moves me forward rather than remaining stuck in neutral or frozen in uncertainty and fear. A metaphor I envision is this: I think of my passions and strengths as the ship I sail on, my fears as a treacherous reef that threatens to wreck my ship, and my values as the towering lighthouse that guides me as I navigate the precarious seas of life. I often face unfortunate circumstances and hard choices; no one is immune from difficulty. When confronted with a hard choice, I will feel much better about my decisions when

1. I understand my core values, strengths, fears and passions,
2. I've chosen an option that leverages my strengths and passions and isn't in conflict with my values,
3. I understand the meanings I give to my actions.

Simply put, I would never have tried something as bold as a triathlon had I not done some major soul searching first. I certainly wouldn't have been able to finish my races without having asked myself to identify my deeply personal reasons for undertaking such a grueling challenge.

Despite all these lessons I've learned in triathlons, my biggest challenge still lay ahead. All this life and business experience achieved outside the confines of my family home still did not erase that little voice in my head that told me that I would never be good enough when dealing with certain members of my family. I would soon be reminded that within my family I was still "just danielle" and my voice was not being heard.

Part 3—The Journey to Owning My Powerful Voice

TRAUMA AROUND THE TABLE

*The single biggest problem in communication
is the illusion that it has taken place.*
— George Bernard Shaw

Beginning in 2014, my parents and eighteen members of our family began having "family meetings." These took place at either my parents' place or my sister Patricia's place in Quebec. The group included my parents, all five daughters, our husbands and all our children. Twice a year, we would come together to discuss family values and stories, financial literacy, cybersecurity and, through a trivia game and memory card game I created, our shared family history. My four siblings and I also began meeting amongst ourselves more frequently to discuss our vision and to prepare for the role of ownership and managing financial assets once our parents are no longer with us. We called these "sister meetings". And finally, my sisters and I began meeting annually with our parents at their home in Florida in formal gatherings we call "council meetings," where we discuss in detail estate planning, finances and legal documents.

It all sounds really healthy and open, right? That was certainly the culture we were trying to create. When we first conceived of all these meetings, I imagined them as an opportunity to celebrate what we'd achieved as a family in the past and to plant seeds for future growth.

March 2016 marked a pivotal point in my life. My parents, my four sisters and I were having one of our council meetings in Florida. I had been in the field of family legacy for almost four years and had come a long way in building up my expertise in family enterprise. (Enterprising families are families who have a shared interest in managing something together, be it a family vacation home, investments, philanthropy, a business and the like, and have an aim to pass it along to subsequent generations.) I was gaining an understanding of the discipline through readings, conferences and talks, university wealth programs and reaching out to other enterprising families to ask questions about what did and did not work for them. I had also become a member of The Investment Group for Enhanced Results in the 21st Century (TIGER 21), a global peer-to-peer networking and education group for high-net-worth investors. In other words, I knew what challenges families like ours faced and I wanted to share that wisdom.

In the course of my studies, I read Patrick Lencioni's business book *The Five Dysfunctions of a Team,*[11] which outlines five hurdles teams have to overcome in order to reach their full potential. They are the following:

- Absence of trust. Teammates must have enough confidence and faith in each other to say what needs to be said, especially when it's uncomfortable and/or makes them feel vulnerable.
- Fear of conflict. This includes letting stuff slide, fostering "artificial harmony" and allowing mediocre to be good enough. Teammates must face conflicts and keep communicating through the pain, remembering that they are all in this together.
- Lack of commitment. Teammates have to be steadfastly dedicated to the shared goal and work together to build and maintain momentum as they pursue it.
- Avoidance of accountability. There is a lack of ownership in the goal and the action steps to achieve it. Teammates must know what everyone is responsible for and hold themselves and one another accountable.
- Inattention to results. This means lack of a dashboard and benchmarks. Teammates have to "know the score" at all times or they can't tell if they're making progress.

In considering these five dysfunctions of a team, I saw that they could be applied equally well to a family that works together—a family like my own. I thought deeply about this and decided to share my learnings with my parents and sisters at our upcoming meeting. I had no specific plan other than using my voice to share what I knew. I spent the ensuing weeks creating a vision for how best to be of service to my family. I spent countless hours painting a perfect picture in my head. I was excited to bring my knowledge to the table and be part of the stewardship of my parents' legacy, most notably in the crafting of a hundred-year plan that would truly honour all the hard work my dad had done to bring us to where we were. I believed that we could overcome the proverbial curse of "shirtsleeves to shirtsleeves in three generations"—a proverb I came across that drove me forward to learn more. I knew time was of the essence; my parents were not getting any younger. By some estimates, 70 percent of high-net-worth families lose their fortunes in the second generation and over 90 percent lose them by the third. That 90 plus percent failure rate speaks volumes about the dynamics that lead to these results.[12] These were the stats I was coming by at the time. I didn't want that to happen to us. I wanted to know all I could so that my girls were not the third generation of wealth transfer who would lose it all. What did I need to know to preserve and grow all that was built by my father and his father? This was the question that drove me forward.

The proverbial saying of "shirtsleeves to shirtsleeves" has been translated and heard in cultures around the world:

- In Lancashire, northwest England—"Clogs to clogs in three generations."
- In Italy—"From the stables to the stars and back to the stables in three generations."
- In Spanish—"Who does not have it, does it; and whoever has it, undoes it."
- In China—"From peasant shoes to peasant shoes in three generations."
- In Japan—"The third generation ruins the house."
- In Mexico—"Father merchant, son gentleman, grandson beggar."
- In Brazil—"Rich father, noble son, poor grandson."
- In Australia—"From goon to Grange to goon."
- In Britain—"Sandals to sandals in three generations."

As far back as the 1700s, this idea can be found in Dryden's *Fables Ancient and Modern*, where he writes, "Seldom three descents continue good." The information I came by pointed out that wealth was depleted as it transferred hands from one generation to another. Rarely was there success, and that happened only if the assets were managed well and the transition to the next generation was handled right.

Newer studies in the field, as reported in an article by Dr. James Grubman, Dr. Dennis T. Jaffe and Kristin Keffeler,[13] had the opportunity to retain the beneficial elements of what was learned over the past forty years, shedding any underlying pessimism and refocusing on a more positive, purposeful and professional orientation in what they coined Wealth 3.0. Wealth 3.0 adds greater emphasis on intrinsic motivation—the desire to create a good outcome simply because it's the right thing to do. It's driven by purpose rather than fear. Holding family meetings, teaching financial literacy and creating foundations for the family's values and collaboration can all still be done. And they can be propelled by an innate desire for engagement, mutual trust, respect and shared values.

All this to say that by my awareness of shirtsleeves to shirtsleeves, I was driven forward to learn what can work best for my family to preserve, grow and create a culture of stewardship within our family and through the generations. The key for successful transition was more than well-drafted documents and great financial and legal paperwork. The real key for successful transition was communication and common purpose.

I would compare this transition to a baton being passed to the next runner in a relay race.[14] At one point, both generations hold the baton at the same time, before one lets go and cheers on the runner for the next leg of the race. It's not the end, just the next phase. Too many enterprises treat the handoff like the flip of a switch without a much-needed period of support. If either generation is not prepared, then it's remarkably easy for that baton to fall and for an established family to lose wealth and face.

Unlike public firms, family-owned businesses have the advantage of shared culture, purpose and values, also identified as the "familiness factor," that give them a unique competitive advantage. A PricewaterhouseCoopers survey in 2018 showed that businesses run by a founder tend to experience double-digit growth, and they tend to outperform the efforts of the second generation.[15] Those that continued to grow at more than 10 percent attributed that success to having a "clear sense of agreed values and purpose."

You can only reach that critical stage by having open and honest communication between the generations. This is best achieved by creating a strategic plan together and reinforcing it via family meetings. The composition of the board of directors is also key to future success. As baby boomers enter their retirement years, we are about to see an enormous transfer of wealth in the next few years, moving businesses to a rising generation at a rate that we have never seen before. However, if the person stepping in as the new leader is not ready, or there is not a strategic approach to the next phase, that precious baton could easily be dropped.

As David Bentall writes in his book *Dear Younger Me*, "Both generations require an appreciation of the needs of the other and ought to be actively considering how they may assist one another."[16]

I knew we could succeed as long as my sisters and I were sufficiently prepared for our parents' wealth transfer, and I also knew that open communication between the generations would be the key to our success. As I anticipated the coming council meeting, I gathered steam like a train filled with hope, gratitude, learnings, goodwill, optimism and faith. I was so eager to share with my loved ones a vision for moving us closer to being the kind of family that everyone would want to emulate. I had no way of knowing that my "Little Engine That Could" was about to be derailed and come to a crashing halt.

At this particular meeting, I was using my confident voice. Remember, I was always quiet at the family table. Using my voice with confidence was something that was far outside my comfort zone, especially within my family setting. I knew what I was talking about and that gave me courage. I spoke with confidence to my parents and sisters, knowing that what I was saying was for the good of the whole family. I asked my parents some questions, most notably whether or not they were willing to share with us the contents of their will. I'd learned that an essential element of legacy planning is to prepare the children (with their youngest being forty-three at the time) to receive the wealth. I knew that if we sisters were to be good stewards of our parents' legacy, then each part of the plan—including the amount of proceeds at stake and especially our parents' intentions—needed to be disclosed and analyzed. In fact, I thought that all our wills should be brought to the table and discussed, otherwise our plan would be a fragmented hodgepodge and probably would not be strong enough to stand the test of time.

When I was done speaking, I thought I'd stated my case for transparency and openness quite convincingly. Then the hammer dropped.

The reply from my father was clear.

"No. Not now."

I know that wills are personal and can change over time, yet the information contained within them truly represents the cornerstone of our planning. I pointed out once again that we put our family's legacy in peril by not bringing them into the light and discussing them. As I continued with confidence and tried to clarify my position, my father suddenly pounded his hand on the table and, in a thundering voice, shouted, "Danielle, are you not grateful for *anything*?"

I felt as if my heart had been ripped from my chest. My first thought was, You're questioning my gratitude? I looked to my mother and siblings for support as they sat in stunned silence. The emotion I felt was so strong, I could not stay at the table any longer. It was not a safe space to be vulnerable, to show my emotions or to express how hurt I was.

As I said in earlier pages, I left the table, closed myself in the washroom and cried as I've never cried before. I could not stop, and I didn't want to stop the uncontrollable sobs that washed over me. I let the tears flow and my body shake. Nobody came to check on me. Although I felt alone in that moment, I knew that my sisters stood up for me and were considerate enough to leave me space to recompose. We sisters always have one another's backs. Slowly, my crying subsided. I composed myself and returned to the table.

Before sitting, I spoke these words to my father: "You thinking that I'm not grateful has really hurt me." At that, I sat and endured the rest of the meeting in silence.

That meeting was my ultimate defining moment.

After I returned home from that meeting, I thought at length about what had happened. Upon much reflection, I decided that

I was responsible for this conflict for several reasons, most of them based on a lack of clear communication. It was a hard pill to swallow.

First of all, my father—and probably the rest of my family, too—was not accustomed to me being a voice at the table. Who was I to question all the work my parents had spent so many years documenting? Clearly, he felt that I had crossed the line of respect. Second, I did not make clear my core intention, which was to grow and connect deeper as a family and to preserve the wealth my father laboured so diligently to build. All the hard work put into preparing for the meeting, all the excitement about the role I was ready to assume and the time I was ready to sacrifice to help the family through the next steps—it was all so clear to me, yet it was a mystery to everyone else. The vision was mine and mine alone, and that was a sobering thought.

I had failed to paint the picture so that my loved ones could see it. Because they could not see it, they could not support it.

I realized that everyone has their own perspective and that I had only considered my own. I had been working countless hours, creating my ideal vision and having such clarity in my head about how the conversation would unfold. I did not include anyone in this process, which left me seeing what no one else could see. Here again was a time when communication and collaboration would have been key to moving forward as a family unit. I had failed at engaging my family in this process. I was a lone wolf and did not include the pack. The final reason I was responsible for the blowup was I had not given sufficient voice to my gratitude for everything my parents have done for me. I thought I'd showed it in other ways whenever I was with them; however, they needed more. They needed the phone call. They wanted to hear my voice literally saying to them, "Thank you,

Mom and Dad, for everything you've done for me." I had not given them that gift, and I deeply regretted it.

I felt extremely low at that moment in my life. I had been like a balloon inflating myself with ideas, yet these ideas were just internal to me. No one else was affected or inspired by them. I was afraid the balloon would pop; I would fall and there would be no one to catch me.

I was alone. Always alone. Always misunderstood.

I'd move forward thinking I was doing a good thing and then— *wham!*—something would come from left field to knock me off my feet. I meant no harm to anyone. I always tried to see the good around me. Nonetheless, there were times—like that meeting in 2016—when I felt so much judgment that I was paralyzed.

As I sifted through these harsh realizations, I was left wondering: Who am I, really? Why am I here and does my being here even matter? What role am I playing in this lifetime I've been given? How can I even begin to make sense of it all?

And so began my journey to find the root of what was holding me back so I could grow into my true self and own my powerful voice.

LIFTING THE MASK OF "NEVER GOOD ENOUGH"

When you change the way you look at
things, the things you look at change.
—Wayne Dyer

Trying to get to a core understanding of who I am and how life's defining moments have shaped me has been similar to peeling off the layers of a pungent onion. There have been more than a few tears shed, that's for sure. My journey has been an emotional one that has required total honesty—about how others have treated me and more importantly, how I have treated myself. I've come to realize that all my life I avoided taking this sort of deep inner dive because the deeper I went, the more I was forced to abandon long-held beliefs about myself, my loved ones and my circumstances. This was uncomfortable, difficult work. And, the degree of difficulty was no excuse for shying away from it. I can think of nothing more difficult—nothing more heartbreaking, really—than to arrive at the end of life and realize that I have squandered the opportunity to gain some understanding of what it all meant.

> *We sacrifice our health in order to make wealth, then we sacrifice our wealth in order to get back our health. We are so anxious about the future we don't enjoy the present. The result being we don't live in the present or the future. We end up feeling like we're never going to die and then die never having truly lived.*
>
> — Dalai Lama

As I processed all this, I began to flash back to the defining moments of my life—my little classmate's rejection after my bout of stage fright in the Christmas program, the clash from the New Girl's question in tenth grade, my mother's lack of trust in me when it came to my interactions with boys, my cousin's hesitance to give me a business card after months of hard work, that awful family meeting when my father questioned my gratitude, and other similar incidents. I realized that I had been reinforcing negative perceptions about myself for the majority of my life. In fact, I had accepted them as gospel and imagined that I deserved them.

By telling myself these hurtful stories over and over again, I had given them power over my mind, body and spirit. That's why I began describing myself as "just danielle" in sad little lowercase letters. My emails were signed with a little *d*. I did not share my perspectives and remained quiet, thinking my point of view mattered to no one. I was going about my life believing that I could be nothing short of perfect, especially when being a voice at the family table. It's why I avoided conflict at all costs and rarely spoke my truth about anything, especially when it was contrary to what my loved ones or authority figures wanted to hear. It's why I clammed up and sat alone in the shadows, watching everyone else play together in the sunshine. It's no surprise that I was so unfulfilled.

One of the most impactful celebrations of my life represents a grand turning point for me—the kind of turning point that I hope you, too, will experience. It happened for me at the Scone Project in Scotland, which I described at the start of this book. This was the program where each participant made a mask symbolizing our most significant limiting belief about ourselves. I described the making of the mask at the outset. I haven't yet told you how the story ended.

The 2016 Scone Project had twenty participants of next generation leaders with an age range of twenty to forty years old. Participants came from all over the world. We had an impressively facilitated program for five days where we explored our roots, embraced the present and our values, exposed our vulnerabilities and had a blank page to write the next chapter of our story by creating our own personal success plan. It was an opportunity to connect with the person we want to be and define how we want to show up in our home, our family, our workplace and beyond.

The Scone Project was hosted by William Murray, Viscount Stormont, in Scone Palace, a lovely historic castle in Scotland. The scenery was surreal. The palace was built in red sandstone with a castellated roof. The grounds included a collection of fir trees and beautiful gardens. Peacocks and Highland cattle welcomed me. Upon entry, I was transported through Scottish history and was filled with appreciation that this would be my home for the next five days.

In my opening pages, I shared how working on my mask was similar to watching an old Polaroid photograph develop. With each embellishment I applied, the picture of my limiting belief came into sharper focus until at last, I held in my hands the mask that said it all. Although it was cheerful and bright and covered with sparkly stars and feathers, I had written in bold letters across the front these three damning words: NEVER GOOD ENOUGH.

After we made our masks, the facilitators encouraged us to sit quietly for a while and simply feel whatever we felt as we looked at them. It was a sobering experience for me. I sat at the long craft table surrounded by all the other participants and held my little mask with the bright feathers and sparkly glitter and the terrible words NEVER GOOD ENOUGH plastered across the forehead. The mask stared back at me with empty eyes and with a power that cut right through me. As my tears fell, I remember thinking, Damn it, this is not what I want for myself! I no longer want to believe that I am not good enough. At the conclusion of the exercise, the facilitators told us to take our masks back to our rooms and keep them there, because they wanted us to wear them to a ball to be held later in the week.

I'll never forget how I felt standing in front of the mirror on the appointed evening and putting on my mask before heading downstairs to the ballroom. Shame for feeling so bad about my-self. Regret for all the time I'd wasted beating myself up. Anger for all the painful moments that had brought me to this low point. I experienced a literal flood of feelings.

I was terribly uncomfortable as I stepped from the privacy of my room to make my way to the ballroom, muttering internally as I walked, Is this the way I want to go forward every day for the rest of my life? Feeling like a failure? Feeling like a fraud? Hiding behind a mask feeling like I'm not good enough?

When I entered the ballroom and saw all the other participants wearing similar masks covered with terrible words describing their self-perception—doubt, no one will listen, rejection, judgment, not deserving of love, failure, fear, hurt, not worthy—I felt a profound shift in my heart and in my soul. All the shame, regret and anger were washed away, and I was overcome with compassion—for them and for myself. I realized I was not alone in this awful feeling of inferiority; we are all in this humanity thing together. I wasn't thinking only of those of us at Scone Palace that night, I was thinking about *all of us*, everywhere. I wanted to run through the room and yank the mask off every person. I longed to hug them mightily and tell them how beautiful we are, how strong and capable, how great and magnificent and extraordinary, inside and outside and all around!

The Scone Project participants and guests, Scone Palace, Scotland, 2016.

After a few minutes of mingling, the facilitators told us that if we wanted to, we could take off our masks. Everyone wanted to.

Oh, my goodness, what liberation I felt when I finally removed mine! In that glorious moment, for the first time in my life, I accepted that I too am beautiful, strong, capable, great, magnificent and extraordinary—inside, outside and all around. I felt freedom and the lightness of being truly who I am, all that I am—authentically me. I had no need to hide behind a mask anymore. Here I am! This is *me*!

Joyous laughter filled the room as we all celebrated our liberation together. After a few moments, the room became a little quieter as we collectively relaxed into our new normal. You know how it feels when you arrive home after a long and exhausting trip? It was kind of like that. It was like a blessed homecoming, like a reunion with myself.

As the ball ended, the facilitators encouraged us to return to our rooms to journal about one strength we wanted to focus on going forward and how we wanted to present ourselves in the world from now on. Sitting at my desk with pen and paper, I was so excited and so optimistic as I thought about all the possibilities. My pen was flying across the pages of my journal. My writing couldn't keep up with my whirlwind thoughts. The bottom line is my voice matters, and I am enough.

The following day, we gathered by a fire for one last celebratory ritual. We had been told to bring our old limiting belief, the words we attached to our masks, written on a piece of paper. One by one, we stepped up to the fire and tossed our limiting belief into the flames. One by one, we saw our false belief turn to ash and be taken up by the wind. There was immense depth to this act. The symbolism, the action, the metaphor all combined to make a powerful point: I am not this false story. I am not this limiting belief. I am not inadequate. I am truth personified. I am limitless. I am powerful. And the choice to step out of the shadow and into the sunlight is mine.

I choose to be *enough*.

I choose to live in the light and share it with everyone I meet.

I choose to be present, to show up fully and to nurture a heart filled with love—for others and for myself.

Now that I'd named what I was feeling (inadequate, insignificant, never good enough) and knew why I felt that way (because I'd repeatedly told myself negative stories about my self-worth), I wondered what I—a mature woman well into her fourth decade of life—could do to change all this. They say that you can't teach an old dog new tricks; as a dog lover, I know that's not true. So, I decided to try a straightforward experiment. Instead of reinforcing tired old stories about my weakness, fragility and naïveté, I would begin telling myself new stories about my strength, wisdom, beauty and worth and see if it made a positive difference in my outlook and behaviour. And so began my process of self-discovery.

Keeping My Saboteur at Bay

> *Our doubts are traitors and make us lose the*
> *good we oft might win, by fearing to attempt.*
> — *William Shakespeare*

When I was eighteen and still living at home with my parents, I had a beautiful husky named Gonzo. On occasion, she would wander around our street, visiting one or more of our neighbours, entertaining them and comforting them and pretending she belonged to them. She was quite the loveable vagabond. At some point in the afternoon, I would receive a call from the neighbours asking me to come pick her up. I had the idea to attach a sign to her collar that read, "Dog for hire. Call this number should you wish to experience the joy of having a dog for the day!" I also considered starting a dog-walking service in my neighbourhood since I loved dogs and I also wanted my own income. I may be part of an affluent family, but cash in my pocket had to be earned and was not easy to come by. In our household, we daughters had to make our own. At first, the dog-walking opportunity seemed like a winning proposition all the way around. I didn't follow through because my prevailing thought was, my parents can't have a daughter who does that. My perceptions were skewed because I felt I could not measure up to the success that surrounded me.

I had many similar ideas for activities I thought might bring me joy and fulfillment, yet they never measured up to what I imagined my parents expected of me. Consequently, I tossed aside any idea or action that felt like anything less than a grand achievement. At the time, the only thing I knew I could accomplish with any success was to be obedient.

Once I left the shadow within my family home, when I married in the year 2000, I grew beyond these limiting beliefs and began to embrace many life challenges, from travel to triathlons. I learned to leap at the opportunity to face a challenge and to persist when obstacles arose as I mastered new skills. (I have an example of this in the pages to come when I performed at the Kiwanis Music Festival.) When I stumbled, as I often did, I learned from the experience. The critical voice inside my head had gone quiet . . . until I was back under the branches of my family tree.

Virtually everyone has this type of inner "saboteur." Author Rick Carson attached this label in his book *Taming Your Gremlin* since this little voice sabotages our attempts to become whole by deliberately disrupting, delaying or destroying our success.[17] How much weight I gave to my saboteur had a huge impact on the attitudes I engaged when I looked out at the world. The impact on my mindset and attitude had an effect on my behaviour, my actions and therefore my results. If I did well, I opened my mind to better days ahead. If not, I began a negative cycle of blame and lower expectations. Once these negative thoughts took over or held back my voice (as they did for me as a child), I began to shrink from risk, avoided new experiences and deprived myself of some of the great joys in life. Just being aware of the influence of my thoughts could lead to finding ways to overcome those limiting beliefs.

A Matter of Mindset

> *Challenges are what make life interesting.*
> *Overcoming them is what makes life meaningful.*
> — *Joshua J. Marine*

Everything is a matter of perspective. I recall the story of two shoe salespeople who were sent to a developing nation to explore business opportunities for their company. One came back to the home office reporting there was no opportunity there since people don't wear shoes. The other sent back a message: "Great news! Lots of opportunity here. No one has shoes!" It all comes down to perspective and state of mind. What state do you want to live in? A rich state filled with opportunities for growth, or a bleak state seeing only closed doors?

For years, I had chosen one where others around me drew the lines, and I lived within them. That was not going to happen anymore.

I thought of the times I had the choice to look at the world through the lens of either a fixed or a growth mindset. Having a fixed mindset, I believed I could only go so far, so there was no point in trying to reach new horizons. I decided at an early age to mentally limit my aspirations, even if it was a dog-walking business. If I faced criticism, I blamed someone else or deflected the barb, ignoring any valuable kernels of wisdom or insights I could have gained. My goal was to keep an upper hand without taking risks or else I may expose a weakness. As a result, I felt threatened when others succeeded and resorted to judgment when the world didn't fit my expectations. This defensiveness meant I consistently tried to cover up my shortcomings (real or perceived). In my view, in this instance, the world is binary; I was either smart or dumb, a winner or a loser, enough or not enough.

Ultimately, my mindset—whether it was open to learning or limited by judgment—determined how much effort I put into new ventures. This is about my outlook, rather than my intellect. When I saw more potential value in my efforts, I pushed myself further forward. How empowering it was to feel that momentum without holding myself back with my own limiting self-image. By ripping off my mask, I freed myself to see so much farther and clearer. I'm determined to help others do the same by whichever technique works for them.

I sometimes use the analogy of the "scarcity versus abundance" mindset, where I either feel the world is against me or there is ample opportunity to succeed. I prefer the "saboteur versus sage" model as I continue to try to quell my own nagging little voice. The saboteur aims to merely *survive* in the world while processing a series of negative emotions, such as anger, regret and blame. The sage looks to *thrive* while being curious, calm, grateful and empathetic.

By listening more to my sage side, I draw on an inner coach within the innovative problem-solving part of my brain to guide my thoughts and actions. I can train my brain to be more sage than saboteur by focusing on situations where I have been in command and performed well—no matter how tempting it was to replay my clumsy moments or missed opportunities. Also, I become more sage when I surround myself with positive people and ask myself questions that open me up to finding my way through a decision or a process. Most importantly, I talk myself up so I feed myself positive thoughts that give me more energy and hope.[18] Once I believed I could learn and grow continually, I committed more of my mind to that process as I sought out my full potential. Ultimately, I found inspiration whether I succeeded or not, which propelled me to achieve more and have more control over—and happiness within—my life.

As soon as I could learn to stop hankering for my parents' approval (or lack of disapproval), I could take more risks and recover more quickly from setbacks. I began to cultivate new talents and take more risks. Obstacles just became temporary problems that did not define me.

I can barely describe how liberating this was. I was proving to myself that mindsets are learned and can be changed. For example, there's a big difference when I tell myself, "I have failed" versus "I'm a failure." By learning and committing to doing things differently next time, I grew into someone who finds more happiness in life.

Don't just believe me on the power of this outlook. Carol Dweck, a psychologist at Stanford University, sets out four steps to changing your mindset, which reflects what I learned in the mask-making and mask-burning exercise in Scotland:

1. Learn to hear your fixed mindset voice.
2. Recognize you have a choice.

3. Talk back to it with a growth mindset.
4. Take the growth mindset action.[19]

You can have fun with this exercise to make it stick in your mind, as some of my coaching clients have done with great success. One of them tells me that whenever an old negative self-judgment pops into her mind, she envisions the judgment as a little dark cloud swirling angrily over her head. It is followed closely by a fluffy, smiling white cloud that symbolizes her opposing positive affirmation (growth mindset thoughts). As my client speaks her affirmation, she imagines the white cloud taking in a deep breath of clean cool air and then blowing the dark cloud away. *Poof!* She's instantly back on track.

Another one of my clients came up with a fun, two-stage process. Once he'd identified he wanted to work on self-judgment, he decided to picture his saboteur as a scowling, overpowering judge with a gavel in his hand. Whenever this client realized that he was being hard on himself, he envisioned this judge pounding the gavel sharply on the table. This image helped him recognize harmful self-talk, although it didn't seem to empower him to overcome the judgment. Instead, it closed him in and made him feel small. Then he learned to visualize the hard wooden gavel as a little yellow and red plastic toy that squeaked every time it came crashing down. *Squeak!* instead of *Bam!* Judgment no longer had the power it once had. My client now smiles whenever he passes judgment on himself and can say, "I know better than that!"

Another person I know visualizes a devil on one shoulder and an angel on the other. As the devil whispers negativity into one ear, the angel proclaims the opposite into the other ear. The angel always prevails.

Yet another client imagines the negative belief as an ugly little rat that she picks up by the tail and drops into a wooden box. As she gives voice to her growth mindset, she sees herself putting the lid firmly on the box and walking away from it. She says she can hear the rat frantically scratching on the inside of the box, trying to get out, and that somehow motivates her to keep walking away from the negativity. Hey, whatever works!

There is great power in these visualizations and in being able to name your saboteur and change your mindset. Once named and recognized, you have the power to keep it small and not allow it to take over your every thought. If you are not sure when your saboteur shows up, question its presence every time the words "should have, could have, would have" cross your mind. The saboteur is part of you and can never be fully eliminated. With the right tools and determination, you can continually take action to keep it in the back seat and allow your true captain—your highest, most glorious self (your sage)—to step up and take the wheel.

I tell my clients that a journey of self-discovery is a lot like designing their estate plans. Circumstances are always changing. There is always more to do. My expedition to myself has been the same bumpy and winding road. I sometimes struggled to stay in a positive state. Common sense is not common practice. Keeping myself moving in a clear and comfortable direction seemed to require more navigation skills than I had. For example, I often caught myself yearning to hear other people tell me my strengths. Not hearing anyone validating them made me believe I didn't have any. My saboteur really played with this. Therefore, I had far too many moments in which I felt that everything I was doing was wrong and that I lacked the power to change. In other words, my progress was not as quick and fluid as I wanted it to be. However, I kept trying and this skill grew stronger over time. It was like training for a different type of triathlon in life.

This process reminds me of the parable of the good wolf versus the bad wolf. It goes something like this:

> An elder was teaching his young grandson about life. "A fight is going on inside me," he said to the boy. "It is a vicious fight between two wolves. One is evil. He represents anger, envy, sorrow, regret, greed, arrogance, self-pity, guilt, resentment, inferiority, lies, false pride, superiority and ego. The other is good. He represents joy, peace, love, hope, serenity, humility, kindness, benevolence, empathy, generosity, truth, compassion and faith. The same fight is going on inside you and every other person."
>
> The grandson considered this silently for a moment and then asked his grandfather, "Which wolf will win the fight?"
>
> The elder replied, very simply, "The one you feed."

In short, I have the power to decide which wolf I'm going to feed and which voice I will amplify. It truly is up to me. The choice is mine and mine alone. No matter what my voice tells me, I give myself permission to be human. When I get a negative trigger, it is normal for my mind to go right to judgment. The question is, do I get stuck there, or do I have the resilience to move forward and seek out the learner's path? As executive coach Marilee Adams says, "Change your questions, change your life."[20] Curiosity is the only antidote to a fixed mindset.

Okay, perhaps changing your self-talk script is not as simple as I've made it sound, especially after decades of diligent negative reinforcement. Old habits die hard, and they do die when you install new habits in their place. It just takes time, commitment, willpower and perseverance.

Talking My Way to Empowerment

> *The heart of a man is very much like the*
> *sea. It has its storms, it has its tides, and*
> *in its depths it has its pearls, too.*
> — *Vincent van Gogh*

With that in mind, I resolved to start small. I had wanted to overcome my stage fright after facing such humiliation at that Christmas concert in grade three. Whenever my daughter Olivia was scheduled to play her violin at a Kiwanis Music Festival or in a recital, I would learn the piano portion and accompany her as she played. I did this until she became such an advanced violinist that I wasn't sure I would be able to keep up with the complex arrangements. Olivia played fearlessly while I fingered the keys with absolute terror. I could deal with messing up on my own but being the cause of my daughter's failure would be devastating. It would have been like freezing up in the elementary school Christmas program. I didn't want to repeat that traumatic experience.

So, I started doing two things differently. First, instead of shying away from the stage, I repeatedly put myself in situations where I had to perform in front of a crowd. What better way to achieve this goal than to pair myself with another peer again. I bravely agreed to perform a violin duet at the Peterborough Kiwanis Music Festival with another mother. She and I practiced and practiced as I built up my confidence. Yet, at the final rehearsal before the performance, when one child after the other played their songs so beautifully, I was hit with a case of the nerves. I began doubting my ability and started to shake. Playing the violin with shaking hands does not work. The bow did not hit the strings as it should have, and my sound reflected my lack of confidence. I'm not sure what I was playing; it was not music. My duet partner stayed calm and held the melody while I moved shakily forward. We made it to the end; however, the question on everyone's mind was whether I would be able to perform well at the festival. Second, I started using the power of self-talk.

Determined to get over this fear and prove to myself that I was capable, I kept practicing. By these actions, I showed myself that I did know my music and that I could play beautifully. I said to myself, why should it make a difference whether I have an audience? Let me play because I love to play and because there is joy in making music. I also used a trick I had learned called "Up Until Now." It works like this: When trying to overcome a long-standing difficulty, I say to myself, "Up until now, I have had stage fright. I don't have stage fright anymore. Beginning right now, I am calm and confident onstage." If I said this "Up Until Now" phrase often enough, I would free myself from a limiting belief that had been holding me back. I would remind myself that people and circumstances could change; in fact, they change every minute of every day. Nothing about my personality or behaviour has to be carved in stone.

Mindset matters. If I believed I was not good at something, I used the "yet" concept too. Simply adding "yet" to the end of my negative belief gave me some leeway while still committing to my goal. For example, I began saying, "I'm not good at playing in public *yet*." Anytime I told myself or I heard my children say, "I can't do that," I added the word "yet," and the mindset changed. The truth was, with effort and practice, I could be good at anything. I just needed to be patient and keep trying. As the proverb says, practice makes perfect. And with determination, anything was possible.

I am happy to report that my intense practice, coupled with my "Up Until Now" mantra, worked like a charm. My fellow violinist and I played at the festival perfectly in tune with each other. To disconnect myself from the watchful gaze of the crowd and to really connect to the music, I played with my eyes closed. Feeling the lovely sounds that were being created by our two violins, I thoroughly enjoyed the moment. I did it. We did it. The music was great! It was so much fun, we played again the following year. How powerful it was to overcome an obstacle such as that. I now know that I can achieve whatever I put my mind to.

Although closing my eyes was a last-minute decision on my part, I could have warned my duet partner in advance that there was a possibility I was going to do it. When she glanced over and saw me with my eyes closed, she thought it was because she had misplayed the music. Never underestimate the power of communication!

Cue Good Communication

> *The most important thing in communication*
> *is to hear what isn't being said.*
> — *Peter Drucker*

Communication is one of the most important life skills to develop, and I never felt like it was one of my strengths, especially after the family meeting where my father misinterpreted my intentions as ungrateful. Clear transmission of my thoughts and desires enables me to pass information on to other people and to understand what is said to me. Communication is a two-way process where I develop a shared understanding of knowledge being transmitted and received. If done well, it decreases false interpretations, allows for greater perspective and builds trust and relationships.

If only I had read the signs from my father's body language better, I could have picked up on his frustration before he banged his fists on the table. After all, communication is more than the words we speak. Tone and body language play a part in communication as well. Most experts agree that 93 percent of all communication is nonverbal. There's a concept called the 7-38-55 rule,[21] based on the communication of emotion. The rule states 7 percent of meaning is communicated through spoken words, 38 percent through tone of voice and 55 percent through body language. Listening is also a vital skill to communication that most people take for granted. Listening is not the same as hearing. It was for me a skill worth mastering. I have two ears and one mouth for a reason. Meanwhile, my shoulders, eyes, arms and other body parts speak volumes as well.

My work as a Family Enterprise Advisor introduces families to being intentional about what and how they communicate. Making money is hard work. Keeping it and transitioning it to the next generation is even harder. Communication brings the gift of certainty about how to proceed when decisions need to be made by someone other than the wealth creator. In my desire to understand why wealth is unsuccessfully transferred beyond the third generation, I learned that much of it is due to a lack of communication. As Thomas Deans states in his book *Willing Wisdom*, "Silence is the greatest destroyer of wealth."[22]

If my family knew that I was preparing a new vision for them, they could have prepared to hear it and brought their own ideas to share. By focusing more on *why* I thought it was vital, I may have engaged them in a more constructive way. On the upside, my hard-earned lessons have paid off by giving me the experience that can help other families navigate these difficult waters. How's that for taking on a positive outlook?

Next Come New Habits

> *You'll never change your life until you change*
> *something you do daily. The secret of your*
> *success is found in your daily routine.*
> —John C. Maxwell

While all forms of communication are vital, my internal dialogue made a big difference as well. Creating a new habit of substituting negative stories about myself with positive ones became my next focus. To do that, I had to focus on adopting some new habits. Research tells us that it takes an average of sixty-six days for a behaviour to become a habit.[23] At first, that sounded like too long to wait for my reward of feeling better, then I considered the alternative: a lifetime of feeling unfulfilled. In my view, it was worth investing the time and effort to create a new habit of positivity.

More than 40 percent of the actions I took were governed by habit, not actual decisions. Yet, if I approached them with purpose, my habits could change if I knew how the brain worked. Just ask anyone who has succeeded on a diet or has quit smoking. "You can't extinguish bad habits; you can only create new ones!" says Charles Duhigg in his book *The Power of Habit*.[24] The habit loop follows three steps: a cue that triggers the brain to go to automatic mode; a routine based on a physical, emotional or mental activity that comes from the cue; and a reward that tells your brain whether or not the loop is worth remembering. According to Duhigg, willpower is essential to success and habit change. To transform a negative habit, you go through these stages:

1. Identify the old habit.
2. Identify why it feels comfortable.
3. Identify the cue.
4. Use the same cue.
5. Identify the new routine.
6. Create a better reward.

For example,

1. Old habit—making a mistake when under pressure, then berating myself
2. Craving—hearing the voice of my familiar inner saboteur
3. Old cue—feeling inadequate
4. New cue—acknowledging the presence of my saboteur
5. New routine—dispersing negative thoughts by reframing them
6. New reward—trying again, then getting it right

New habits were easier to form if they were aligned with my previous routine. I would also have far more success if I made a plan to create my new habit by anticipating obstacles and working around them. Finding someone to hold me accountable for my new approach also helped. (I will discuss the value of that process soon). In the meantime, I stayed focused on my future goal. I continued on my new path to stay motivated and be kind and patient with myself as I incorporated new things into my life. I was determined to break myself free from the chains of my perceived insignificance and inadequacy once and for all. That is how daily affirmations became part of my life.

The Power of Affirmations

> *Once you make a decision, the universe*
> *conspires to make it happen.*
> — Ralph Waldo Emerson

Just like reinforcing good habits, I could set myself up for staying on track by reminding myself of my inner power. The best way to beat back my inner saboteur was to create a proactive system to quell that voice. That meant feeding myself regular doses of words that reinforced what I was capable of accomplishing to keep up my energy and focus. This practice was impressively effective and set me up for a better outlook each time I told myself I could. The more inspirational the message, the better.

Imagine that your dearest friend has come to you in tears, telling you that she is giving up on ever finding a lasting romantic relationship. She explains that she has gone out with several guys over the past few months, yet they always stop calling after a couple of dates.

"I think it's because I'm so boring," she says. "I'm a terrible conversationalist. I never know what to say, so I just sit there like a bump on a log. Nobody wants to be with someone as dull as me. Mom always told me that I needed to lighten up and quit being so stodgy, and she was right."

That's quite a negative story your friend is telling herself, isn't it! How would you respond? Would you say, "Yes, Sally, your mom is correct. You are a world-class bore. Being around you is like sinking to the bottom of the ocean. You really should give up on ever finding love"?

Instead, I'd tell her that she is a delightful, kind and attractive woman with much love to give. I'd remind her of all the times she was the opposite of dull, including all the times she made me laugh or taught me something new. In short, I'd do everything in my power to tell her a different and more positive story, one that encourages her and helps her feel better. If I can give this gift so lovingly and openly to a friend, why then, can't I give it to myself? Affirmations/incantations are simply a form of self-talk that lifts me up and motivates me to be my best. There is nothing silly or wrong about that.

To "affirm" something is to declare that it is true. In the context of self-development, affirmations are statements of truths that I want to draw deeply into myself and my life, truths whose energy I want to absorb wholeheartedly and, ultimately, pass on to others. To generate the most impact, I repeat them aloud or silently, over and over again, until they become an integral part of who I am. For these affirmations to work, I check in with myself and make sure they pass the so-called gut test to ensure my words feel authentic. To make a change, the affirmation (or what I also call an incantation) must involve the mind, body and spirit. Knowledge is not enough unless I act upon it.

Here are a few examples of affirmation statements:

- I am filled with energy and joy.
- I am courageous.
- I am a strong person who stands up for myself.
- I come from the source of love and light. I am love and light.
- I am at peace.
- I am a voice that matters.

Notice that these statements are focused on me in the now, not in the future. This is an important distinction. Author Gary John Bishop writes in his book *Unfu*k Yourself: Get Out of Your Head and into Your Life*:

Assertive self-talk is when you stake a claim for this moment of time, right here and now. When you start to talk in terms of "I am..." or "I embrace..." or "I accept..." all of which are commanding uses of language rather than the narrative of "I will..." or "I'm going to..." the physiological and psychological impact of using in-the-moment, assertive language is not only powerful, it has a very real in-the-moment effect. There's a massive difference between "I am relentless" and "I will be relentless." One of those statements intervenes in this moment of your life, the other lives more like a description of what's to come rather than what's here.[25]

Some people balk at creating affirmations for themselves because they think it's silly to say that they're something they're not. For example, take the affirmation "I am courageous." Is it wrong to tell myself that I'm courageous if I'm not? My first response to that question is, what makes me so certain that I'm not courageous? I can assure you that deep down in my psyche, I possess profound courage. Perhaps in my present circumstances I'm not feeling particularly brave, not yet. My innate courage is still there waiting to be tapped into. Acknowledge it and bring it forth! Every time I declare that I'm courageous (or joyful or strong or whatever), I rewire my brain—and the energy of the universe—to make it so. Just as doing physical exercise builds and strengthens my muscles, repeating affirmations builds and strengthens my spirit. When I make positive and empowering statements a habit, I interrupt the cycle of negativity and break free from my self-imposed limiting beliefs. In other words, I remove that nasty mask.

The moment I started creating my affirmations, I felt a discernable shift in my attitude. I knew that I was onto something, and it was going to be good. I began by making a list of my limiting beliefs and judgments about myself. As I wrote my list of negative thoughts about myself, I let the heartache of my saboteur's judgments wash over me. I experienced the pain fully, with the confidence that it was about to become a much less dominant force in my life. Then, beside each limiting belief, I wrote an opposing positive statement that would become my affirmation/incantation.

Here is my actual list:

My limiting beliefs	What I've moved to
My voice does not matter.	My whisper plants seeds that grow into great things.
I am insignificant.	I am essence itself.
I am not good in a crowd.	My presence is powerful.
I am failing as a mother.	I am the best mom my girls have.
I do not connect with people.	I connect deeply with others.
I am always misunderstood.	I am articulate.
I cannot handle conflict.	I am courageous and face my fears.

To remind myself of my strength and inner power and to bring forth my true self, I practice saying my positive affirmations, out loud and silently, every day. It has become a habit that I look forward to. Sometimes I say them in the shower. Other times, I say them while I'm driving or running on the treadmill. And—this is important—I say them whenever one of my old limiting beliefs crosses my mind.

In working on my own development and helping other people with theirs, I've learned that there is no step-by-step process to follow. The journey is different for everyone. If I had to pick a few steps that virtually everyone can benefit from, they would be as follows:

1. Remind yourself that life happens for you, not to you.
2. Remember that there are no problems, only gifts. It's all in the meaning we assign to the stories we tell ourselves.
3. Make a habit of voicing affirmations. Just as you would encourage a dear friend, you can—you must—encourage yourself. Why not give it a try? Speak it loudly. Speak it from a place of full truth and watch your spirit soar!

I live in a much more fulfilled state now. The best part is that the experience inspired me to get into legacy and resilience coaching so I can help other people come up with healthier ways of looking at themselves and their circumstances. This is especially true for people like me from affluent families where it's so easy to get lost in the shadows of our family.

As I help my clients find their light by substituting their limiting stories with encouraging affirmations, their radiance rebounds and shines on me. What a precious gift—leaning into my truest self! This light is like an electric circuit with no end. It starts with taking care of myself. Once my well-being is in harmony, I can give back and be the difference in my family, the community, my coaching clients, my family enterprise advisory clients and the world. It's an energy of positive change all around. What I give is returned exponentially.

Eventually, I realized that if my "good wolf"—my sage—was ever going to be strong enough to ward off my pesky and persistent "bad wolf"—my saboteur—I was going to need someone other than me to hold me accountable for feeding her. Instinctively, I knew that to achieve the results I wanted now and to grow into a stronger mentor for the next branch of the family tree, I couldn't do it alone.

It was then that I turned to my first coach for assistance. Spoiler alert: it was the best decision ever!

HOLDING MYSELF ACCOUNTABLE

I'm courageous enough to know I can accomplish great things. I'm humble enough to know when to ask for help.
— Katrina Mayer

For those of us on a path of self-discovery, it's common to get a little beaten down by insecurity from time to time. Sometimes our progress seems too slow. Sometimes we have a setback. Occasionally, despite our best efforts to affirm our strengths, we'll have a nasty visit from our saboteur, who is only too happy to inform us of our shortcomings.

Even I still have occasional setbacks. We travel to Montreal often to spend time with my family, taking our dogs—a West Highland White Terrier named Jojo and a black Portuguese Water Dog named Pademay—with us. On one particular visit in 2018, we left our dogs in my younger sister Sabrina's fenced backyard while we visited with family inside the house. Due to her two miniature poodles' size and resourcefulness, my sister had secured her yard by diligently installing netting to block every little hole and crack so they could not escape.

When I went outside to check on the dogs that afternoon, I noticed a large piece of netting on the lawn. My young Pademay, who had always been so well behaved, had shown her first signs of destruction by clawing at the netting and removing a section of it. I could not believe that my perfect puppy was no longer perfect. Although I didn't see her do it, I imagined she was looking for a way out of Sabrina's safe enclosure. I placed the pieces back as best I could. I felt bad because I knew my sister would have to put in some work to fully restore it. I did not want to admit what Pademay had done, yet I knew I must for the sake of her dogs' safety.

I entered the house to tell Sabrina, then chose not to interrupt the conversations going on at the table. Sabrina's husband's side of the family was also present, and it was a full house. I eventually lost all courage to say anything. As was my pattern when faced with conflict, I shut down. I ended up leaving and began my four-and-a-half-hour drive home without speaking a word of Pademay's crime.

My heart was heavy. I was wrong and I knew it.

I had to call Sabrina and tell her, so I started thinking of how to explain what had happened and why I had neglected to say something earlier. The more time that passed, the more I felt in the wrong, and the conflict in me grew bigger. Just as I was about to dial her number to give her the news, my cell phone rang. It was Sabrina, calling to tell me about the hole in the fence. I acknowledged that my dog was at fault, and I apologized for not saying anything before we left. I'm so grateful to Sabrina for not judging me too harshly as my inner voice screamed at me, "See, she understands! Why did you stay silent?"

I still felt terrible for not having the courage to face the situation. I had been working so hard to start using my voice, and I thought I'd made so much progress. Obviously, I still had work to do. My takeaway from this incident was that old habits don't magically disappear just because I want them to. I have to be diligent and manage my behaviour continually. I used this as a teaching moment for my girls, who were in the car with me and heard my conversation with Sabrina over the car speakers. My message for them was this: When things are left unsaid, misunderstandings happen and are compounded unnecessarily. When you have something to say, say it then and there. When you don't, a perceived fear festers and grows and too often the FEAR is False Evidence Appearing Real.

To this day, I still feel that I lost my sister's trust because of my silence in that situation. I journaled on the importance of transparency after that and vowed to use my voice even when it makes me uncomfortable. Journaling is another tool I used in my journey to self-discovery. Journaling evoked mindfulness and helped me remain present while keeping perspective. It helped my brain regulate emotions and provided a greater sense of confidence and self-identity. I still do not use my voice all the time, yet I have come a long way from being the silent little girl at the dinner table. Sabrina and I have shared many moments throughout our life. We shared rooms as children into adulthood. We raised children at the same time. We learned to ride a motorcycle together. She was with me during many of my first experiences. Whenever I need a pillar to lean on, Sabrina is there. From her, I learned the importance of saying things then and there and that family is always there for me.

Adding a Coach to Your Team

> *A coach is someone who tells you what you don't want*
> *to hear, who has you see what you don't want to see, so*
> *you can be who you have always known you could be.*
> — Tom Landry

Likewise, having a nonjudgmental, skilled, caring and detached coach beside me gave me fresh perspective and renewed empowerment every step of the way. The best thing about working with a coach was the effect it had on perspective and confidence. Thanks to the saboteur, I had learned to think of myself as weak, helpless, incapable, not good enough—if not all the time, at least part of the time. A certified coach, with an International Coaching Federation (ICF) certificate, begins with the assumption that we are all born with the competence, power and wholeness it takes to achieve lasting fulfillment in our lives. They believed that I innately have the resilience to overcome any setback, the wisdom to create any new outcome and the ability to learn whatever I need to know in order to move forward in fulfillment. These inborn capabilities are my birthrights. The coach's tasks guided me as I claimed those birthrights—as I uncovered the strength and competence that was already within me—and helped me face any saboteur standing in my way.

Since the coaches know that I was born to succeed and since they have studied the path of self-discovery, they can help me identify and bust through the roadblocks I encountered on the way back to my authentic self. They would help me develop a scoreboard for tracking my progress and celebrate with me as I made gains, no matter how small they might seem. Understanding my saboteur was essential if I was going to put it in its place (in the back seat, where it belongs). Remember, the saboteur was "the little voice" that puts me in my place as a way of protecting me from impending danger. As described in *Co-Active Coaching: The Proven Framework for Transformative Conversations at Work and in Life,*

> The voice is there to keep you from taking unsafe risks, but it is often overcautious at a time that calls for risk for the sake of change and a more fulfilled life. The saboteur's voice may recite judgment, rules and limiting beliefs, false stories you take as the truth ... Basically the message is that you're not smart enough, attractive enough, wealthy enough, experienced enough, old enough ... you are not enough. Or it could be the opposite: you're too old, bald, frumpy, young, aggressive, introverted, extroverted ... you're too much. Most of the time this voice operates quietly in the background, influencing choices and lobbying for its preferred course of action or inaction. Be aware that whenever people take the initiative to change their lives, an alarm sounds and the saboteur will awaken. Expect it. This is when a coach, a partner you can be accountable to, comes in most handy.[26]

Accountability—what a powerful motivator. Without it, I was left with no meaningful measure of my actions and their effects on my progress. For example, I like to tell myself I'm going to try something new for growth's sake (say, making a habit of affirmations). In the absence of an accountability partner, who provides a framework for these vital steps?

1. Creating a plan
2. Working the plan
3. Reporting on my progress

How could I measure the results? How would I know what's helping and what's not? How would I know when, where and how to pivot to another approach, especially when the saboteur is happy to tell me that I'll never, ever make it?

Once I had my accountability partner, there was no stopping or looking back. The only direction was forward. As a coach of mine used to say, "The way to what you want is not over, under or around—it's going through." From then on, my self-discovery process moved much more quickly and the answers came with less stress and strain. It was great having someone hold me accountable for my actions because actions matter. It's not enough to want to break a harmful, hurtful habit or remove a limiting belief. I had to want it and I had to *act*. Acting is hard when the saboteur has made me doubtful of my abilities and when my perspective has become cloudy. My coaches have helped me stay mindful and achieve clarity on my perspective. They helped me keep the saboteur at bay. Their positive reinforcement gave me the confidence to go forward with courage.

Learn it. Practice it. Live it. This is what I learned alongside my coach.

I also received a boost of confidence when my initial coach, Lisa, noted my high level of emotional intelligence and my ability to speak what I saw. She said there was a quiet power about me; when I spoke about a difficult topic that other people had skirted around, I went straight to the point in a light, calming way that allowed the others around me to speak their truth, too. Her observation motivated me to enter the field of coaching. The accountability continued throughout my learning and certification process with a variety of different coaches. This schooling kept me constantly mentored. I was delighted to discover that this type of work came naturally to me. My career as a coach has turned out to be fulfilling in every way. It is a major part of who I am.

My learnings led me to Yale University Professor Marc Brackett and how he has opened many people's eyes about the value of feelings and emotional intelligence in business and in life—no matter what age they are. As a bullied child, he found solace in the companionship of an uncle who listened to his problems and validated his feelings. From the experience, he learned that his troubles would pass and his emotions about them deserved to be recognized. From there, he developed a blueprint for understanding our emotions and using them to improve the odds of experiencing success and well-being. So often, parents dismiss a child's emotions as a distraction or an unnecessary evil; however, a high emotional intelligence allows you and them to navigate social systems with ease.[27] He's written a great book titled *Permission to Feel*.[28]

This "emotion scientist" does research at the Child Study Center and helped found the Yale Center for Emotional Intelligence. His system, called RULER (**R**ecognizing Emotion, **U**nderstanding Emotion, **L**abeling Emotion, **E**xpressing Emotion, **R**egulating Emotion), reduces stress and burnout, improves school climate and enhances academic achievement. He aims to remove the shame of having and expressing our feelings, unleashing their power so people relate to one another better at school, at work and in life. He focuses on giving everyone the permission to feel. He dives deeper in explaining that emotions are information. I loved his book and learned so much from him.

Tips and Tools for Identifying Your
Authentic Self and Core Values

> *To be a great leader, first become a great person.*
>   *—Robin Sharma*

My experience and my newfound skills particularly helped one of my young clients who came to me in turmoil about his university studies. He had just been accepted to a prestigious MBA program—a goal his father and grandfather, both extraordinarily successful entrepreneurs, had encouraged him to pursue since he was a child. Yet, he could not shake the feeling that he was headed in the wrong direction. He couldn't understand why he felt that way since he'd enjoyed getting his undergraduate degree in business and liked the challenges of the corporate world. When I asked him my series of Bottom-Line Questions about his values, strengths and passions, he described his values as authenticity, creativity and integrity; his strengths as perseverance and optimism; and his passions as art and travel. After some deep self-reflection, he was finally able to admit his fears: that pursuing the MBA would take him away from his passions for art and travel, that it wouldn't be "authentic" since he would be following in the footsteps of his elders, and that going into the family business would stymie his creativity and stunt his growth.

It took a lot of talking and brainstorming, and eventually he realized that it wasn't the idea of a career in business that was bothering him, it was the kind of business. He didn't want to take over the reins of the family company, as expected. He wanted to start his own business based upon his passion for art. Once he understood and accepted this as his truth, he felt the weight of the world lift from his shoulders and his outlook on life shift towards the positive. He summoned the courage to tell his father and grandfather that he intended to become an art dealer, and to their credit, they gave him their blessing.

This happy result arose because my client was willing to ask himself some profound questions and then sit quietly long enough to let the answers come. When the answers came, he was willing to accept them as his truths and courageous enough to use his voice to claim them. With his values, passions, strengths and education now in alignment and his fears alleviated, he was ready to march into a very bright and balanced future indeed, promoting great art to collectors around the world.

When I described the experience of this client and my own feeling of liberation after removing my Never Good Enough mask, I talked about being true to one's authentic self. Those two words carried so much power to guide me on a journey that was true to myself. How did I get started? Let's start by looking at what "authentic self" means.

My authentic self is who I truly am as a person. It has nothing to do with my surname, my occupation, my age, my relationship status or my looks. It goes far beyond how I introduce myself when I meet someone for the first time. To really connect with this part of me, I had to go far deeper. After reading Robin Sharma's *The Leader Who Had No Title*, I realized the deeper my relationships, the stronger my leadership. My motto is built on this philosophy: "Leave every single person who intersects my path better, happier and more engaged than I found them."[29] Time spent forming deep relationships—in all aspects of my life—will pay dividends down the road.

I had to trust myself to follow my own compass rather than the one set by my family, society, culture or the media I consume.

I needed to be attuned to my body, my passions and my ethics. Only then could I accept and embrace my true personality without worrying about whether others would do the same. It's much easier now that I have matured and outgrown the peer pressure of my youth. Being true to myself means loving myself, forgiving myself for errors of the past (real or perceived) and putting myself first. Then I can really follow my dreams without the baggage from other people's journeys.

I can find this beautiful part of me by focusing on my core values. They are a part of me. They highlight what I stand for. They can represent my unique, individual essence. Values guide my behaviour, providing me with a personal code of conduct. When I honour my personal core values consistently, I experience fulfillment. When I don't, I'm incongruent and am more likely to escape into bad habits and regress into childish behaviour to uplift myself. Unfortunately, I started out having not the slightest idea what my core values were. Rather than asking myself quality questions that forced me to dive deeply into my authentic self for answers, I allowed society, family members and the media to dictate my values to me. The result? Confusion. A lack of direction. A feeling of spinning my wheels and getting nowhere. A sense of unfulfillment.

Instead, I focused on what I was told to make the centre of my life: money, prestige, low body fat, a house in the right neighbourhood, a good-looking spouse and the like. On the flip side, I may genuinely appreciate honesty, integrity, exploration of new spaces, freedom from debt, good food or dear friends who may not be in the same social echelon. Only I knew the answer to what truly lit my spark.

Without undergoing a discovery process, it was challenging to identify my personal core values. It's easy to speculate and idealize what I should cherish. Knowing and accepting what I value took effort. When people hear about core values, they often want to select them from a list of personal values. Yet, values aren't selected; they're discovered. I didn't choose my values. My values reveal themselves to me. That is part of their magic.

The good news is that there are tons of tools available to help people identify their values. If you go online and search "Lists of Core Values," you'll be directed to dozens of lists—many of them with hundreds of values to choose from. I even have such a list on my website at DanielleSaputo.com. This can be a fine place to start, especially if no ideas spring to mind immediately. There are also "values cards" in the form of physical decks of cards and virtual ones online that you can sort through to find values that speak to you. Once you've chosen your set of values, you can arrange them from most to least important.

When examining values from a list, I had to be totally honest with myself and select the ones that were sincerely mine, not those I thought I ought to have. This was easier to do when I was guided by a skilled coach who helped me distinguish what's authentically mine and what's not. What I noted was that the goal here was to discover and claim *my* values, not someone else's.

Another tool was to recall my life's most meaningful defining moments. As I saw, they could be times of setback or strife. As I assessed them, I could discern which values would have helped me in those moments (or which values *did* help me, if that were the case). Put another way, which values did I respect and elevate in those moments, or which ones did I smother or set aside for some reason? Within these memories, I would find the qualities of a life lived fully from the inside out. This type of discovery was similar to mining for gold. I have found the examination of my defining moments to be extremely powerful and well worth whatever heavy lifting it took to bring forth the riches.

There was also the discovery of values through questions such as these:

- Beyond food, water, clothing and shelter, what must I have in order to feel whole, complete and fulfilled in my life?
- What kind of person do I ultimately want to be?
- What do I want my life to really be about?

When I answered these questions, I had a set of value descriptors that were authentically mine and not ones chosen randomly from a list. This "values inventory" I've created was quite lengthy. So that I could put my values into action, I needed to narrow them down. Once I recorded my value words, I thought about what each one meant to me. My definition was what mattered here. No one else gets to have a say in this. Then, I held each word in my heart and asked myself: "What has to happen in order for me to feel/express (the value)?" I looked for patterns within the emotions and memories that arose, with the goal of combining many similar values into a single overarching one.

For instance, my list included honesty, reliability and transparency. I felt that those three were related and could be grouped under the umbrella of integrity. Nice! I was able to narrow my focus to one word that really said it all! When I asked myself, "What has to happen in order for me to express integrity?," two answers immediately sprang to mind: "I must speak my truth. I must do as I say." Next, I added respect (I follow the Golden Rule); gratitude (I celebrate the little things); personal growth (I'm a life learner); fun (I love an adventure) and family (I honour my loved ones and our shared history).

With knowledge of my core values and how I would express them, I was able to arrive at my purpose in life: to be a playful, grateful free spirit, enjoying and respecting every connection I'm blessed with and sparking the light of integrity within myself and others so that we all can grow and flourish.

For me, there's no more worthy pursuit than that.

Values may be intangible, yet they are not invisible. People can see them expressed through my actions. By honouring my values and the choices I make in my life, I feel an internal "rightness" that is impossible to ignore. When I know myself and what I stand for, I stand as tall and strong as a mighty sequoia tree and all my positive energy transfers to everyone I meet. Imagine how beautiful the world would be if everyone achieved that level of self-awareness and positivity. I'm doing my best to be there. How about you? If you need a boost, start by asking yourself quality questions and prepare to be inspired by the answers you find within.

Keep Celebrating!

> *Celebrate what you want to see more of.*
> — *Thomas Peters*

Since maintaining a positive self-image was so important on this quest for fulfillment, it was critical to find ways to lift my spirits and keep focused on the present moment. Celebrating even small wins strengthens my well-being and my progress forward. One of the best ways I've found to do that is to give myself something nice, like a trip to the ice cream shop for a treat, a pedicure or an extra hour to relax every now and then to acknowledge and celebrate my successes, no matter how small.

Remember, when you focus your attention on something, it expands. If you want more success in your life, celebrate your success!

I may have to trick myself into party mode at times. I too often move right to the next great thing without taking the time to celebrate the great thing I have just done. In doing so, I lose sight of the fact that I am great! I'm conditioned to acknowledge the major milestones like earning the impressive diploma, winning the big promotion at work or getting engaged to the dream partner. Note that the road to self-fulfillment isn't paved with big milestones; it's paved with little points of light. It's less about the big wins and more about the day-to-day victories that move me forward. Unfortunately, no brass band is going to show up just because I spoke my affirmations every day last week. There will be no community fireworks on the night I summon the courage to use my voice at the family table. The *New York Times* won't send a reporter to write a feature story about my decision to follow my passion for quilting.

No, it's going to be up to me to honour my successes myself. It's up to me to cultivate a celebratory spirit. And sometimes I need a personal champion to help me get there. The coach/coachee connection is a lovely, symbiotic relationship: as the coach lights my way home—warmly, gently, step by glorious step—my light begins to shine a little brighter, too. Soon I'll find myself radiating power and positivity, just as my coach does. This is the kind of synergy that makes life worthwhile and makes the world a better place. Instead of languishing in the shadow, I was growing by drawing others out from within the darkness of their families' shadows. And it felt amazing.

LITTLE SILVER BOXES

Kindness in words creates confidence. Kindness in thinking
creates profoundness. Kindness in giving creates love.
— Lao Tzu

I wish I could remember the name of the speaker who planted the seed back in my university days to do more to get more out of life. I distinctly recall sitting in a lecture hall, listening to the woman. I will always remember what she said. She was talking about goodness in the world and how each of us has the power to expand it by performing simple acts of kindness. Although being kind was not a new concept to me, what she said has stuck with me ever since because of the visual metaphor she used. She described acts of kindness as "little silver boxes" that we give to other people. I love the image of handing someone an exquisite little package and watching their face light up!

When you shovel the snow from your elderly neighbour's sidewalk or cook a meal for a friend who is ill, you're not only relieving them of a chore, you're giving them the gift of love. You're manifesting a wave of goodness that ripples outward from its source and comes back to you like a boomerang. This is especially significant for affluent people. Some of us come to believe that money solves everything (and it does solve some things, of course). I have also learned that simple acts of giving have a bigger impact and result in a greater feeling of fulfillment. Giving is what life is all about. A sincere compliment, a kind gesture, a word of encouragement—these are the precious gifts of love that I can give to anyone at any time. I try to grab those opportunities whenever I can because doing so makes life so much richer.

I seized such an opportunity at the airport a few years ago. I was travelling alone and was awaiting my flight when I noticed some sort of conflict happening at the boarding desk. Another passenger was giving the gate attendant, a middle-aged woman, a really rough time. The stresses of travel can bring out the worst in people, and this passenger was taking out all his frustrations on this poor woman who was only trying to do her job. I have a high level of empathy; it's not hard for me to feel what other people are feeling. When I was a child and saw someone hurt or sad, I'd be right there crying with them. As I watched the gate attendant being dragged over the proverbial coals by the displeased passenger, my heart went out to her. She looked as if she was having the worst day ever. Eventually, mercifully, the passenger finished his tantrum and sat back down.

Boarding began a few minutes later. I took my place in line and slowly made my way towards the gate, watching the attendant as she scanned ticket after ticket. Her body language said it all; her head was down and her eyes were averted. It was obvious that she felt terrible. When it was my turn at the head of the line, I smiled and held out my boarding pass. She took it without looking at me. I was overcome with compassion.

"Excuse me," I said, summoning my courage. "Could you maybe use a hug?"

At that she raised her head and looked at me quizzically. Then her expression softened.

"That would actually be very nice," she replied.

I gathered her in my arms and gave her a nice big hug. By the time we parted, we both were smiling. I thanked her for accepting my hug and told her that she'd just made my day. As I passed through the gate, the gentleman behind me said, "Do I get one, too?" All of us, including the attendant, started laughing. Within seconds, everyone was smiling and some were even hugging. I danced down the tarmac and into the plane. What a way to fly!

That's what life is all about, isn't it? Taking a moment to be mindful of my surroundings and doing one small act of kindness—giving someone a little silver box filled with love—can change the whole atmosphere; yes, for me and for everyone who bears witness. One simple act of kindness does so much for my well-being—yes, for the receiver and the giver as well. As I tell my kids—do good, get good. Whatever I put out into the universe comes back to me in spades. So, I challenge you to give out three little silver boxes today. It can be as simple as letting a clerk know that you like their smile. If you overhear someone say something nice or interesting, compliment them on it. Wave at a passerby. Look someone less fortunate than you in the eye and give them a few kind words. Smile at the person in the car next to you when you're stuck in traffic. Buy a homeless person a meal. The choices are endless.

My learning journey continued, and with each tool and concept I learned, my inner light grew stronger and my true self showed up with confidence and determination. I was coming to know my leader within.

LEADER WITHIN

Experience is not what happens to you—it's
how you interpret what happens to you.
—Aldous Huxley

Now I have a confession to make. Giving out these little silver boxes—especially to people I don't know, like the airport gate attendant, is not as easy as I've made it sound. It is hard for me to put myself out there because I can't predict what the reaction will be. It may be tough for you, too. Nobody likes the idea of being rejected. I'm encouraging you to take the opportunity anyway. I'm confident that once you make this sort of giving a habit, you'll discover that the people around you, in your family and community, have begun following your lead and on and on the goodness will go. Like a pebble dropped into a still pond, the ripples spread further than you can imagine—all because you were willing to take a risk and give without any expectation of a specific return. Giving from the heart is what real leadership is about: inspiring people, yes, by what I say they should do and by my example. The greatest impact is not in catching the fish and giving it to hungry people, it is teaching hungry people how to catch the fish for themselves after I'm gone.

Perhaps you're like me and have not thought of yourself as a leader in the conventional sense. This is typical for those of us from successful entrepreneurial families led by strong, charismatic overachievers. I tend to think of leadership as something the patriarch does while I play on the sidelines or behind the scenes as a team member, without taking the role of the captain. I've learned to be okay with that, for I am my own leader within—strong in my values and my thoughts, leading through action without taking centre stage. After all, the stage is not my favourite place to be despite my best efforts to overcome my performance anxiety. I will find other venues and other ways to act out my role in life's grand opera, thank you very much!

The most effective kind of leadership—the true kind, which I want to express in my lifetime and pass on to my kids—is a continuous act of generosity. It is about:

- Being a mentor, a teacher, a cheerleader.
- Helping people feel good about themselves, inspiring them with their greatness, not my own.
- Encouraging them to reach higher and achieve more than they ever dreamt possible.
- Persevering alongside them, especially when the going gets tough.
- Coaching rather than criticizing.
- Seeing roadblocks as opportunities for growth and learning and getting those around you to see it too.
- Championing collaboration and cooperation.

In other words, it's about believing in them (and myself) beyond reason, thus promoting the notion that we are all inexplicably connected to one another by a greater power and that our connection is grounded in love and compassion. When I accept this notion as my soul's truth, people will be drawn to me like a moth to a flame—a bright, flickering flame fueled by love.

That is the key to building the next generation to lead the family business—not controlling and judging, even via those subtle cues I may not realize I'm sending. Instead, I grow my family's capacity by recognizing that the next branch of the family tree can reach much further. They just need confidence and belief to do it, without being subconsciously held back by the ways "I have always done things."

When I think back to what I once viewed as my parents' overprotection of me, I am less disturbed by it than I used to be because now I understand that just like the rest of us, my parents were doing the best they could with the insights they had. Like you, me and everyone else, they are a product of their upbringing, their culture and their generation. Just as I have my unique perspective on our shared past, they have theirs. They are equally valid and true. Yet another purpose of those painful moments was to teach me how to be the kind of parent who allows—and even encourages—my children to spread their wings and fly. I'm not claiming that this is always easy. On the occasions when I stop to reflect on my lifetime of defining moments and the relationships (both happy and sad) that have brought me to this extraordinary place of love and light, I am overcome with gratitude for all of it. This is true especially for my father, who has propelled me down this road of self-discovery to look deeper within myself than I may have done otherwise, and my mother, who has played her part in shaping the person I am today.

I like to think that the painful moments I've experienced have served a purpose and that is to remind me that there are always at least two sides to every story. Whereas I saw a lack of respect at that family meeting so many years ago, based on my mindset, my father saw a lack of gratitude for all he had done to give me a good life. Gaining perspective has been key to understanding the purpose of my life and finding renewed appreciation for the countless gifts I've been given. When I focus my attention on something, it gets bigger. Its power expands. When I dwell on the pain an experience brought me, I get more pain. Yet, when I turn my attention to the good things I learned as a result of a painful experience, I get more goodness. I get more learning. I get more growth. I grew from the encounter with my dad at the March 2016 meeting, as I did from many other encounters. There is forgiveness and gratitude every time we are together.

It is an incredible feeling to live in a balanced state where I feel my light shining both inwardly and outwardly upon everyone I meet. When I become the kind of leader who gives little silver boxes filled with love, I activate a beautiful contagious feeling of warmth that is passed along from one person to the next. My goal is to help more people reach that state in their lives, to feel their brightness shine. Wouldn't it be lovely if we could have a day when everybody is in that light?

Unexpected Teachers

> *A man in his life may have many teachers.*
> *Some most unexpected. The question lies with*
> *the man himself: Will he learn from them?*
> — *Louis L'Amour*

My mother is not the only one who taught me valuable parenting lessons. I was taking a car service one day from Peterborough to Toronto and back (a three-hour round trip) when I struck up a conversation with Billy, the driver and roadway philosopher.

"Yep, I've had many people riding in my back seat there," he said with a chuckle. "I've heard lots of stories, and there are a couple of lessons I've learned that I love to pass on. The first one is to change the 'me' to 'we.' Nobody is the centre of the universe. We're social animals, we human beings. We need each other. You gotta open your heart and open your arms and not be afraid, because love is what it's all about."

Billy glanced at me in the rearview mirror to make sure I'd heard. I smiled and nodded.

"And two," he continued, "ask your kids for advice sometimes. Not enough of us turn to our children for guidance. You'd be surprised how wise they are. Kids know how to cut through the crap and see things the way they really are. And they'll feel like a million bucks if you ask them what they think you should do."

Ah, there is so much beauty in that wise instruction from this driver! From then on, I began including my girls in my decision-making, and the results have been astounding. When I ask a young person for guidance, I forge a deeper connection with them. I help them feel respected and valued for the insights they bring to the table. I teach them to use their voice and speak their truth. I show them that they matter. And I also demonstrate that it is okay to seek counsel. They will understand that if I can come to them for advice, then they can also come to me. Everyone wins.

As it turns out, my middle daughter had an insightful lesson to share with me about living in a balanced state. Olivia and I are alike in many ways. Most notably, we share a love for adventure, sports, travel and photography. I've taken my girls on trips to many different places. We all have a love for animals, my daughters and I, so there is usually some animal adventure involved in our travels, including snorkeling with the sea lions in the Galapagos; visiting a park with grizzly bears in Vancouver; and numerous encounters with koalas, joeys and crocodiles in Australia. Wherever we go, Olivia is the one who is right on my heels ready to do all the adventures I have planned, without reservation. That brings me to a special adventure we shared in the summer of 2018 when we had an unbelievable adventure of a safari in Kenya.

Ever since I got married in the year 2000, my focus had been predominantly on my family. In 2016, I went back to school to get certified in coaching and spent the ensuing years quite focused on my learnings. I am always looking for meaningful ways to interact with my girls and show them the world. So, when I learned of an opportunity to travel to Kenya in 2018, I thought it would be a great way to reconnect with my girls as well as deepen our bond to our fellow human beings on the other side of the world. I was right. Going to Kenya was a fabulous experience. There was an underlying message of moving from "me" to "we." To make a difference in the world, we must first take care of ourselves. When we are in a state of well-being, giving back to the family, the community, the world, brings immeasurable personal benefits. The profits are boundless.

One morning while on this trip, the organizer invited me and the girls to take an early-morning walk with him. Olivia, my intrepid little traveller, immediately raised her hand to join us. We were accompanied by a Maasai warrior, who served as our protector as we trekked outside the enclosed compound. As we hiked through this beautiful landscape, Olivia listened as we exchanged ideas. I was in search of ways to be of greater service, and our wheels were really turning. I was completely energized by all the possibilities. Could I facilitate families coming on these trips? Could I dedicate my time to empower the women and their senior elders, known as Mamas, as they gain sustainability? Could I be a support and coach to the children leaving their families to bring back knowledge through their education? Could I promote positive mental health and the idea that before you give back there's an important element of self-care? The possibilities felt endless.

Back at the compound, as we were returning to our tent, Olivia suddenly stopped walking, turned to me with a serious expression and said something I will never forget: "Mom, you know we still need you, right?"

Her simple question stopped me in my tracks and tugged at my heartstrings. Here I was, planning My Next Big Thing, thinking that my girls had outgrown their need of me. And here was Olivia to bring me back down to earth. To remind me of the necessity of balance. To caution me not to let the pendulum swing too far away from home—not quite yet. For now, I'm a mother, first and foremost. My girls need me. What a blessing that is, and what a blessing to be reminded by my darling, wise Olivia, who was an unexpected teacher to me that day.

With my daughters, Olivia, Enrica and Aurelia, Barcelona, 2017.

LIVING MY LEGACY

Carve your name on hearts, not tombstones.
A legacy is etched onto the minds of others
and the stories they share about you.
—*Shannon L. Alder*

When speaking of legacy, it means much more than an amount of money or property left to someone in a will. A legacy is what is passed from one generation to the next. In the words of Bestow in *How to Leave a Lasting Legacy*,[30] "Leaving a personal legacy involves more than the financial assets you bestow on the younger generation. A lasting legacy is all about the actions you take during your life and the way actions affect how people remember you." The blog goes on to list ten ways to leave a lasting legacy. I would like to emphasize five of them:

1. Think about everyday interactions: small things matter.
2. Champion causes you are passionate about: make a difference in the lives of others.
3. Have zest for life: there's no time like the present.

4. Pass on your family's history: tell stories about your child-hood, your parents and your grandparents.

5. Be a positive mentor: you will be remembered most by the type of personal interactions you have. Always take time to help when you're needed and make an effort to be a positive force in the lives of others.

Over and above the points above, have all your finances and pa-perwork in order.

I sat in a class where we were asked, "What will be your legacy?" and the following definition by Rasheed Ogunlaru resonated with me: "Legacy is not what's left tomorrow when you're gone. It's what you give, create, impact and contribute today while you're here that then happens to live on." I took a moment to reflect and ask myself, "Will my legacy be one of closeness or distance?"

The following are ten ways you can strengthen your legacy:

1. Always ask for input when making decisions that impact the family.

2. Be open to discussing the reason for the decisions you make.

3. Don't create favouritism between your children, and work at eliminating competition for your favour.

4. Don't label family members.

5. Validate all your loved ones.

6. Build trust with all your family members, especially those who disagree with you.

7. Help others find meaning in things, even in the things you don't find interesting.

8. Lead with compassion. Make everyone's voice matter.

9. Be vulnerable to talk about failures, personal relationships and feelings.

10. Engage in your family's interests. The last thing you want is to ignore these interests while you are living, a mistake that could radically impact their lives after you are dead.

I've been taught all this—taking inventory and trying to gain perspective on lessons—by my family and other people. It has caused me to think about the learnings I want to pass on to my loved ones. Thus, I decided to be particularly mindful of what my words and actions might be teaching those around me—especially my children. As a parent, my primary goal is to raise my three daughters so that they grow into strong and confident women who are well equipped to live joyful, fulfilling, productive lives. With that as my goal, I've worked hard to identify and then teach them the things I think they need to know.

If I were to write a list of the lessons I want to impart to my girls (and my clients, whenever appropriate), it would be the following:

For a Satisfying Work Life

- Find your passion and you won't have to work a day in your life. This requires knowing yourself (as Confucius advises), your interests and aptitudes and having the moxie—the character, determination, willpower and courage—to pursue them despite what anyone else thinks. Work without passion is a recipe for disappointment and regret. Working with passion is the formula for fulfillment.
- Don't try to reinvent the wheel! Look for ideas, mindsets and activities that have worked for other people, then copy them, fine-tune them and make them your own and always give credit where credit is due. Coming from an entrepreneurial family, I have learned that you're stronger

when you can lean on someone else and change the "me" to "we." Trying to do everything yourself leads to burnout, whereas if you build on what already exists, you will be lifted and carried much farther than you could ever have gotten by creating something from scratch. Collaboration is key.

For Financial Stability and Freedom

- Never spend more than you have. Ever!
- Always ask, "Do I need this?" before you spend.
- Negotiate. It's always better to have the extra pennies in your pocket than in someone else's. It's the same as when the order taker at McDonald's asks, "Do you want an apple pie with that?" There is no harm in asking. You may be surprised with what you receive if you only ask!
- Remember that you will never have enough money if money is all you have.
- Keep six wallets. This means a portion of all the money you make will be split as follows:

  ○ Wallet #1—Wealth accumulation (your savings), where you put some money for the distant future into investment vehicles that utilize the power of compounding.
  ○ Wallet #2—Planning and saving, where you build on the anticipation and hard work and time it takes before you purchase something of value. Budget your funds to meet your short-term needs and potential emergency fund.
  ○ Wallet #3—Education, where you set aside money for your continual growth and learning (otherwise known as investing in yourself).

- ○ Wallet #4—Giving, where you allocate an amount of money to be given to a charity of your choice, fulfilling the philosophy and meeting the need to contribute to the greater good.
- ○ Wallet #5—Fun! It is equally important to set aside an amount of funds earmarked exclusively for enjoying the fruits of your labours. Some work and some play every day ... that's the basic formula for life-work balance. Wallet #5 will help you achieve it.
- ○ Wallet #6—Daily expenses that cover your day to day cost of living.

For Healthy Interpersonal Relationships

- Always be kind, live with compassion, love unconditionally.
- Choose each relationship wisely, for all your relationships intertwine and impact the others.
- When you want another person to behave in a certain way, make sure you're behaving that way yourself. You cannot change the actions of another. You can only change your own.
- Love to love, not to be loved. There is a big difference between the two. When you give wholeheartedly without an expectation of receiving anything in return, you are never disappointed. When you give with strings attached, frustration is sure to follow.
- Give, give, give—whether it's compliments, hugs, smiles or encouragement. The power of these simple gifts is extraordinary!
- Be grateful. Notice and enjoy the little things in life because one day you will look back and realize they were the big things.

- Express your gratitude to people who hurt you. Blame them effectively. It's a great exercise to learn to let it go. (Blaming effectively allows you to release the pain of the past and use it as a springboard to your future. There's something to learn, even from the hardest of situations. It's taking the mindset that life doesn't happen to you, it happens for you.)

- Treat others as you want to be treated. Live by the Golden Rule.

- Be diplomatic when speaking of your differences with another person. Listen with an open heart. Agree to disagree when the situation calls for it.

- Ask for clarification and ask again if you must.

- Face conflict head on, because when you don't, it creates FEAR (False Evidence Appearing Real).

- Walk the talk; do as you say. Don't let anything compromise your integrity. It takes a lifetime to build a noble reputation, and it takes only five minutes to lose it.

- Walk the walk. Don't make empty promises—you show something is true by taking action rather than just speaking words.

- When you have a decision to make, turn to your children for advice. The parent-child bond will deepen, and you'll also be the recipient of some great ideas!

- Connect with people. The feeling of human connection is incredible.

- Elders have wonderful stories to share and much to teach. Seek them out with reverence and reap the rewards of their wisdom.

For a Winning Mindset and Strong Character

- Start your day with a positive intention.
- Think good thoughts, speak good thoughts, feel good thoughts.
- Be mindful—a relaxed mind brings clearer answers.
- Acknowledge your inner critic, name it and keep it small.
- Be fearlessly authentic. Be brave. Be you. Have the courage to live your authentic self.
- Be attuned to your inner voice. That's your wise one. Know that you always have the answer.
- Trust yourself.
- Make your inner voice heard. Don't hold back.
- Turn a negative into a positive whenever you can.
- Use words that empower you, like "yes" in addition to "and" in place of the limiting word "but."
- When you think you know something, try to see it from a different perspective just for fun. You'll be surprised how often your mindset changes after doing this.
- Be curious; don't judge. Ask open-ended questions.
- Confront your limiting beliefs with courage. Don't let them stop you.
- Remember that you are where you are meant to be. The powers of the universe work in mysterious ways.

For Essential Self-Care

- Eat well. Feed your body with the highest quality, most wholesome food you can find. Do everything in moderation, though. A scoop of chocolate ice cream now and then is good for the soul!
- Chew your food and chew some more.

- Drink plenty of water every day.
- Keep active. Stretch, exercise, strengthen and relax.
- Rest is equally as important as the activities you do.
- Know your vulnerabilities and share them wisely.
- Speak kindly to yourself, as kindly as you would to your best friend. Don't be your own worst critic.
- Be accountable or find someone who can help you be.
- Keep the fun in all you do.

There you have it: the prescription for a fulfilling life that I am working so hard to convey to my daughters. This will be my legacy. How about you? What lessons have you learned in your lifetime thus far? List them, put them into perspective, pass them on and put them to work crafting a lovely legacy of your own. Be fulfilled by living your legacy.

Conclusion

BE PRESENT, SHOW UP AND LOVE

Someone I loved once gave me a box full of darkness.
It took me years to understand that this too, was a gift.
—Mary Oliver

I tell you these stories of lessons I've learned from my life to illustrate that we—you, me and everyone else—are surrounded by teachers, and very few of them will be found standing behind a podium in a lecture hall. I've met the majority of them as I go about my day-to-day life. I'll find them in the checkout line at the grocery store. I'll find them sitting next to me on the subway, driving a cab, asking if I can spare a dime, cleaning my hotel room, helping me renew my driver's license or serving me a meal at my favourite restaurant. And yes, I'll find them in my own family. So, pay attention. Stay alert. Be mindful to the many "teachers" who have a lesson to offer.

Be on the lookout for shifting perspective, for new ways of seeing and doing things. Experience the joy of growing, and don't be so hard on yourself. There's a beauty in going forward in curiosity versus judgment, living in your heart and not in your head.

And remember that just because someone is challenging you on the one hand doesn't mean they aren't also holding a gift for you in the other.

The journey back to myself has been like a gradual unfolding. It reminds me of the cycle of the moon. There are times when I'm in the shadows and feel almost invisible except for a sliver of a line on a clear dark night. Having the title of "Administrative Assistant" printed on my business card after I'd spent so many successful months dealing with salespeople on telecommunications, security and the company's unused buildings plunged me into such a darkness. The same thing happened when my husband referred to me as his "secretary" when he was incorporating and asking me to do his billings. There was also the time my sister identified me as a "housewife" to the prestigious TIGER 21 group when I was applying to join.

I know in my bones I'm much more than any of those labels. I'm a business school graduate with an additional diploma in institutional administration. I won the entrepreneur competition in university and put on seminars for fledgling entrepreneurs, so of course I'm more than just an administrative assistant, a secretary and a housewife. I tend to define myself by the work I do and by what I am paid to do. Until recently, when I was asked, "What do you do, Danielle?" I had no quick answer. My saboteur, my inner critic, my bad wolf, my gremlin—whatever term I want to use for that little voice that speaks limiting words to my subconscious—belittled me, again.

I am nothing. I am insignificant. I am worthless. I am empty. I am not enough.

It is then that I know I must stop and reflect on the answers to my Bottom-Line Questions and remind myself of my values and my Reasons Why. I must reconnect with my accountability partner—my coach—and ask for help. I must start taking better care of myself physically, emotionally, mentally and spiritually. I must celebrate every little victory.

I must watch my language and notice the character traits and feelings I want to bring forth—being more outspoken and feeling confident that I am enough. I can't say that everything has fallen into place and my life is now perfection and completely fulfilled. I can say that my outlook has gotten better and continues to improve.

And when I do these essential things, I soon find that I'm full again—like a full moon—and my brilliance shines and my light touches everyone I meet. Remember, all the darkness in the world cannot put out the light of a single candle. It will shine. Like that candle, I have found my light and it can never be extinguished.

I know who I am.

- I am a mindful mother. Even when I'm overwhelmed at my desk in my home office, I'm always prepared to give my girls my undivided attention should they pass by and need something from me. I will be there for my girls as long as they want and need me, and even longer.
- I am a loving wife. Through the ups and downs, I always carry love in my heart.
- I am a grateful daughter. I will be present for my parents and let them know I'm thankful for all they have done and are doing, even when there are differences of opinion. Especially when there are differences of opinion.

- I am a courageous sister. I will hold on to the values of sisterhood and the strength of unity even when faced with conflict. Especially when faced with conflict.

- I am a connected family member and friend to many as a godmother, aunt, cousin, niece, neighbour, team member, fellow musician, colleague, alumna, cohort and buddy. I will stay connected and use the power of words to share my learnings and knowledge whenever someone shows interest—and sometimes even when they don't!

- I am a grounded inheritor. I manage my wealth and keep learning how to be wise with money. I also actively prepare my children, the next generation, to manage their future wealth. You're never too young to start this training. I know that from experience.

- I am a leader of integrity. I lead by example with honesty and strong moral principles. "Leader" is not a position or a title I have; it is an action and example I live.

- I am an adventurous traveller always booking My Next Great Adventure with the goal of continuing to grow by discovering new places and cultures. This opens me up to seeing things through a different lens.

- I am a legacy-minded photographer. I enjoy capturing moments in time and gifting them later as the memories that make life worth living. I especially love summarizing the year just passed in photos, which I give to my loved ones every Christmas. The greatest joy in doing this is seeing everyone with my scrapbook project in hand, slowly flipping the pages, remembering forgotten moments with smiles on their faces.

- I am a harmonious musician. I play the clarinet in a community band and mentor young musicians. I enjoy filling my home with music by playing the piano and violin too.

- I am a determined athlete who swims, cycles, runs, hikes, skis, skates, paddleboards and keeps active however I can. I am determined to remain flexible and strong. My experience as a triathlete has been a great gift, reminding me that it takes more than physical strength to run this race called Life. It takes strength of character and persistence.

- I am a genuine nature and animal lover. I enjoy watching wild animals in their natural habitats, and I love having pets. I love experiencing life in the company of animals.

- I am a crafter achieving balance. Whether it's stained glass, quilting, pottery, drawing or painting, I love to create art because I see it as essential to a balanced life. I also enjoy observing and supporting artists at work.

- I am a pursuer of knowledge, a life learner always ready to gain new insight and try something different.

- I am a trusted family advisor, holding family clients accountable for having intentional conversations. Encouraging conversation leads to better connections, stewardship and family harmony.

- I am an authentic coach helping other people rediscover their authenticity. Being accountable together on this shared journey to our deeper selves—what a gift for me!

- I am a joyful daydreamer. I have so much in my head that always works out so well, it makes me happy and content.

- I am a dedicated volunteer willing to lend a helping hand wherever I can. My volunteer efforts nurture my mind, body and soul.

- I am a fun-loving, free-spirited motorcycle rider. I love to spend the day, especially as the sun sets, riding scenic roads. The experience is even more fulfilling when I'm part of a group of people who share my love of riding.

Yet at the same time, I am a lone soul at peace with myself. I ensure that I have much quiet time for reflection, during which I often dream of being in a cabin in the woods surrounded by water and mountains, where I read, think and write, alone in the company of a loyal dog.

I am Danielle Saputo. My mission is to be present, show up and love, and *I am enough*.

As we now part ways, I wish you the fulfillment of your personal mission in life, whatever it may be. May you walk in the sunshine with your head held high, and know that you, too, are always enough.

Notes

1 Jennifer Williamson, *Sleep Rituals: 100 Practices for a Deep and Peaceful Sleep* (Simon & Schuster, 2019), www.aimhappy.com.

2 All client interactions are kept confidential. Names and other identifying factors have been changed to protect privacy.

3 Suniya S. Luthar, "The Problem with Rich Kids," *Psychology Today*, Nov. 5, 2013, https:// www.psychologytoday.com/us/ articles/201311/the-problem-rich-kids.

4 Luthar, "The Problem with Rich Kids."

5 Marianne Williamson, *A Return to Love: Reflections on the Principles of "A Course in Miracles"* (HarperOne, 1992).

6 Dr. Kevin Leman, *The Birth Order Book: Why You Are the Way You Are* (Baker Publishing Group, 1998).

7 Jocelyn Voo, "Birth Order Personality Traits: Your Guide to Sibling Personality Differences," *Parents*, July 30, 2020, https://www.parents.com/baby/development/social/ birth-order-and-personality/.

8 Kahlil Gibran, *The Prophet* (Alfred A. Knopf, 1993).

9 Tony Robbins, *Awaken the Giant Within: How to Take Immediate Control of Your Mental, Emotional, Physical and Financial Destiny!* (Simon & Shuster, 1992).

10 See the full context in the excerpt in "Living Up to the Family Name."

11   Patrick M. Lencioni, *The Five Dysfunctions of a Team* (Jossey-Bass, 2002).

12   Study by John L. Ward of Northwestern University's Kellogg School, 1987.

13   Dr. James Grubman, Dr. Dennis T. Jaffe and Kristin Keffeler, "Wealth 3.0: From Fear to Engagement for Families and Advisors," *Trusts and Estates*, Feb. 2022.

14   Danielle Saputo and Jeff Helpern, "Family Enterprise Decision Tree", July 2022. https://familyenterprise.ca/resource/decision-tree/

15   PricewaterhouseCoopers, Global Family Business Survey 2018, https://www.pwc.com/gx/en/services/family-business/family-business-survey-2018.html.

16   David C. Bentall, *Dear Younger Me… Wisdom for Family Enterprise Successors* (Castle Quay, 2020).

17   Rick Carson, *Taming Your Gremlin: A Surprisingly Simple Method for Getting Out of Your Own Way* (Harper Collins, 2003).

18   Sarah Bedrick, "The Ultimate Guide to Mastering Your Mindset [in 10 Steps]," Thrive Coaching, https://www.thrivecoaching.io/how-to-master-your-mindset/.

19   Carol Dweck and David Yeager, "Mindsets: A View from Two Eras," *Perspectives on Psychological Science*, Feb. 1, 2019, https://www.ncbi.nlm.nih.gov/pmc/articles/PMC6594552/.

20   Marilee Adams, *Change Your Questions, Change Your Life: 10 Powerful Tools for Life and Work* (Berrett-Koehler, 2009).

21   Albert Mehrabian, *Nonverbal Communication* (Transaction, 1972), 133.

22   Thomas William Deans, *Willing Wisdom: 7 Questions Successful Families Ask* (Détente Financial Press, 2015).

23   Phillippa Lally et al., "How habits are formed: Modeling habit formation in the real world," *European Journal of Social Psychology* 40, no. 6 (Oct. 2010): 998–1009.

24   Charles Duhigg, *The Power of Habit: Why We Do What We Do in Life and Business* (Doubleday Canada, 2012), 112.

25 Gary John Bishop, *Unfu*k Yourself: Get Out of Your Head and into Your Life* (Harper Collins, 2016), 168.

26 Henry Kimsey-House et al., *Co-Active Coaching: The Proven Framework for Transformative Conversations at Work and in Life* (Nicholas Brealey, 2011), 114.

27 Marc Brackett, *Permission to Feel: Unlocking the Power of Emotions to Help Our Kids, Ourselves, and Our Society Thrive* (Celadon, 2019).

28 See chart below. From *Permission to Feel* by Marc Brackett (Celadon, 2019).

Enraged	Panicked	Stressed	Jittery	Shocked	Surprised	Upbeat	Festive	Exhilirated	Ecstatic	▲
Livid	Furious	Frustrated	Tense	Stunned	Hyper	Cheerful	Motivated	Inspired	Elated	HIGH ENERGY
Fuming	Frightened	Angry	Nervous	Restless	Energized	Lively	Excited	Optimistic	Enthusiastic	
Anxious	Apprehensive	Worried	Irritated	Annoyed	Pleased	Focused	Happy	Proud	Thrilled	
Repulsed	Troubled	Concerned	Uneasy	Peeved	Pleasant	Joyful	Hopeful	Playful	Blissful	▼
Disgusted	Glum	Disappointed	Down	Apathetic	At Ease	Easygoing	Content	Loving	Fulfilled	▲
Pessimistic	Morose	Discouraged	Sad	Bored	Calm	Secure	Satisfied	Grateful	Touched	
Alienated	Miserable	Lonely	Disheartened	Tired	Relaxed	Chill	Restful	Blessed	Balanced	LOW ENERGY
Despondent	Depressed	Sullen	Exhausted	Fatigued	Mellow	Thoughtful	Peaceful	Comfortable	Carefree	
Despairing	Hopeless	Desolate	Spent	Drained	Sleepy	Complacent	Tranquil	Cozy	Serene	▼
◄——— LOW PLEASANTNESS ———►					◄——— HIGH PLEASANTNESS ———►					

29 Robin Sharma, *The Leader Who Had No Title: A Modern Fable on Real Success in Business and in Life* (Simon & Schuster, 2010), 220.

30 Bestow, "How to Leave a Lasting Legacy," Apr. 1, 2019, https://www.bestow.com/blog/how-to-leave-a-lasting-legacy/.

For Further Study

The more that you read, the more things you will know.
The more that you learn, the more places you'll go.
— *Dr. Seuss*

Just like the food we eat, the media we consume has a profound effect on our health. When we ingest material that urges us to think of ourselves as powerless victims, we become discouraged and frozen in fear. And when we consume positive material that encourages us to reach higher, we become empowered, motivated and energized. We shine! The following are some wonderfully positive videos and books that I've found helpful in my life and also in my coaching and advising practice. I recommend them to you wholeheartedly and hope they inspire you as much as they have done for my clients and me.

Recommended Videos and Podcasts

- Brené Brown's TED Talk on Listening to Shame: https://www.youtube.com/watch?v=psN1DORYYVo

- Brené Brown's TED Talk on The Power of Vulnerability: https://www.youtube.com/watch?v=iCvmsMzlF7o
- The Dalai Lama: Rules of Life: https://www.facebook.com/CurejoyInspirations/videos/707346259458651/?video_source=permalink
- Edison's mother's genius: https://www.youtube.com/watch?v=cwghlYxY6kE
- Friedman's Theory of Differentiated Leadership Made Simple: https://www.youtube.com/watch?v=RgdcljNV-Ew
- James Rhee's TED talk on Kindness: https://www.ted.com/talks/james_rhee_the_value_of_kindness_at_work
- Shawn Achor's TED Talk on The Happy Secret to Better Work: https://www.ted.com/talks/shawn_achor_the_happy_secret_to_better_ work?language=en
- Simon Sinek's TED Talk on How Great Leaders Inspire Action: https://www.ted.com/talks/simon_sinek_how_great_leaders_inspire_action?language=en
- Tony Robbins on Letting Go of Fear: https://www.tonyrobbins.com/podcast/letting-go-fear
- Where are you?: Conscious.is/video/locating-yourself-a-key-to-conscious-leadership

Recommended Books

- *The 5 Love Languages: The Secret to Love that Lasts* by Gary Chapman
- *The 7 Habits of Highly Effective People: Powerful Lessons in Personal Change* by Stephen R. Covey
- *Aged Healthy, Wealthy & Wise: Lessons from Vibrant and Inspiring Elders On How They Designed Their Later Lives* by Coventry Edwards-Pitt

- *The Anatomy of Peace: Resolving the Heart of Conflict* by Arbinger Institute
- *Awaken the Giant Within: How to Take Immediate Control of Your Mental, Emotional, Physical and Financial Destiny!* by Tony Robbins
- *The Birth Order Book: Why You Are the Way You Are* by Kevin Leman
- *Build a Lasting Legacy: What it Takes to Connect Your Family for Generations* by Bhaj Townsend
- *Change Your Questions, Change Your Life: 12 Powerful Tools for Leadership, Coaching, and Life* by Marilee Adams
- *Carry On, Warrior: The Power of Embracing Your Messy, Beautiful Life* by Glennon Doyle Melton
- *Children of Paradise: Successful Parenting for Prosperous Families* by Lee Hausner
- *Co-Active Coaching: The Proven Framework for Transformative Conversations at Work and in Life* by Henry Kimsey-House, Karen Kimsey-House, Phillip Sandahl and Laura Whitworth
- *Cross Cultures: How Global Families Negotiate Change Across Generations* by Dennis Jaffe and James Grubman
- *The Cycle of the Gift: Family Wealth and Wisdom* by James E. Hughes, Susan E. Massenzio and Keith Whitaker
- *Dear Younger Me ... Wisdom for Family Enterprise Successors* by David C. Bentall
- *Eat That Frog!: 21 Great Ways to Stop Procrastinating and Get More Done in Less Time* by Brian Tracy
- *Every Family's Business: 12 Common-Sense Questions to Protect Your Wealth* by Thomas William Deans
- *Family Fortunes: How to Build Family Wealth and Hold on to It for 100 Years* by Bill Bonner and Will Bonner

- *Family Wealth: Keeping It in the Family—How Family Members and Their Advisers Preserve Human, Intellectual, and Financial Assets for Generations* by James E. Hughes
- *The Gift of Failure: How the Best Parents Learn to Let Go So Their Children Can Succeed* by Jessica Lahey
- *The Gift of Imperfection: Let Go of Who You Think You're Supposed to Be and Embrace Who You Are* by Brené Brown
- *I Will Not Die an Unlived Life: Reclaiming Passion and Purpose* by Dawna Markova
- *The Leader Who Had No Title: A Modern Fable on Real Success in Business and in Life* by Robin Sharma
- *Life Is What You Make It: Find Your Own Path to Fulfillment* by Peter Buffett
- *Loving What Is: Four Questions That Can Change Your Life* by Byron Katie and Stephen Mitchell
- *Nonflict: The art of Everyday Peacemaking* by Amir Kfir and Stephen Hecht
- *Permission to Feel: Unlocking the Power of Emotions to Help Our Kids, Ourselves, and Our Society Thrive* by Marc Brackett
- *Raising Financially Fit Kids* by Joline Godfrey
- *A Return to Love: Reflections on the Principles "A Course in Miracles"* by Marianne Williamson
- *Rooted in Family: Honoring the Past While Creating Our Future* by Caroline Coleman Bailey
- *Safe Space: Governance in Action* by Francesco Lombardo
- *The Seat of the Soul* by Gary Zukav
- *Silver Spoon Kids: How Successful Parents Raise Responsible Children* by Eileen Gallo and Jon Gallo
- *The Soul of Money: Transforming Your Relationship with Money and Life* by Lynne Twist
- *The Speed of Trust: The One Thing that Changes Everything* by Stephen M. R. Covey

- *Strangers in Paradise: How Families Adapt to Wealth Across Generations* by James Grubman
- *Taming Your Gremlin: A Surprisingly Simple Method for Getting Out of Your Own Way* by Rick Carson
- *The Ultimate Gift* by Jim Stovall
- *Unfu*k Yourself: Get Out of Your Head and into Your Life* by Gary John Bishop
- *Willing Wisdom: 7 Questions Successful Families Ask* by Thomas William Deans

For Help Finding a Professional Coach or Family Advisor

- www.DanielleSaputo.com
- The International Coach Federation: https://coachfederation.org/find-a-coach
- The Co-active Training Institute: www.coactivenetwork.com
- Family Enterprise Canada: https://familyenterprise.ca/

Acknowledgements

Writing a book is a dream I never thought I would fulfill and here I am fulfilled in so many ways. I'm eternally grateful to my first contact on this journey, Pamela Suarez. You listened, you heard and through you, my words were put to paper. Without your skills so much would have remained thoughts in my head or many scattered thoughts in journals. Thank you for the first great step to the legacy I now have to share.

Moving me forward and putting in the time to read my manuscript and give me feedback are these treasured souls:

Olivia Geloso, your feedback is always welcomed. You have keen insight. I thank you for being a voice of truth and encouragement. You are fuel that keeps me going.

Lydia Saputo, you always have kind words to say. Even in your productive criticism you have me strive to be my best self. Thank you for seeing this in me and for your continual encouragement.

Barbara Chisholm, your suggestions and comments kept me inspired. Feedback like yours kept me courageous to keep this project going.

Chantal Bouillon, you have inquisitive questions. You add perspective that makes every conversation with you rewarding and thought provoking. Thank you for your friendship and honest openness.

Massimo Venturino, your comments were like the wind in my sail. You added momentum and your feedback has pushed me to publish my work. Thank you!

Richard Voss, your perspective adds a welcome point of view. Thank you for taking the time and giving me exactly what I asked for. Your feedback was received with much appreciation.

Vincent Didkovsky, you gave my work the final sweep, cleaning up the last typos and you uncovered more that that. Thank you for seeing me as a wise, confident, friend, who you would come to for advice. The same is for you.

To my first hired coach and dear friend, Lisa Cantelon, who has the great ability to have me see past my saboteur. Thanks to you I found the ability to lead without a title and be authentically me. You've planted the seed to have me push past my limiting beliefs and thanks to you I pursued and achieved. I'm grateful to you!

To Jennifer Williamson, you warmed my heart with your quick and open response when I reached out to you for the use of your poem. Not only did the words I read touch me, you also touched me deeper with your encouragement and the kind words you gave so freely to a stranger. Thank you!

A special thanks goes to Jennifer Tiberio for her talents in turning my first manuscript into something amazing. All your input has driven me forward with excitement.

To Kirby Rosplock, Julie Morton, Wendy Sage-Hayward, Tom Deans and James Grubman for your wise words, being mentors and endorsing my work.

To Ann Kornuto for encouraging me through the steps of promoting my book on social media.

To everyone who replied to those posts and kept me excited through the process.

To Lois Tuffin, Leslie Schwartz, Diane Rush and Donna Dawson for taking me a step further in editing my work.

To David Wogahn and your team for helping me through the steps to publishing.

Thank you!

About the Author

Danielle Saputo is a life learner dedicated to bringing out the best in herself and others. Danielle earned a bachelor of commerce and a graduate degree in institutional administration from Concordia University. She completed wealth management courses at the University of Toronto's Rotman School of Management and The John Molson School of Business in Montreal. She is an Accredited Certified Coach through the International Coaching Federation (ICF) and The Coach Teaching Institute (TCTI) with designations in emotional intelligence, resilience and legacy coaching. She also trained with the Co-Active Training Institute (CTI) group in co-active coaching. She is a designated Family Enterprise Advisor (FEA) through the Family Enterprise Exchange and a Certified Applied Positive Psychologist (CAPP) through the Flourishing Center.

As a professionally trained Co-Active Coach and ICF Certified Resilience and Legacy Coach, Danielle's goal is to help her clients re-imagine their lives and let go of negative thoughts and undermining behaviours so they can emerge renewed and fulfilled. Specializing in leadership and family enterprise, Danielle helps members of affluent families to step out into the sunshine and live their most meaningful and authentic lives. With extensive coaching experience and a vast history of client success, her personal commitment is to provide her clients with accountability, understanding and support on their journeys of self-discovery. Her coaching mission is to help every client live his or her legacy with confidence. As a family advisor she is clarifying purpose, resolving conflict and amplifying clients' total wealth. Through open dialogue and reflective questions, Danielle strengthens connection, trust and harmony.

Danielle worked in her family's business until she married and began a family of her own. She is president of Danuto Holdings and manages investments. On the home front, Danielle organizes and leads family meetings, creates multigenerational games and coordinated the writing of a family values book. Her focus is on building a family legacy and fostering financial literacy and stewardship in the next generation.

Danielle has a passion for travel, animals, nature and staying active. She enjoys the tranquility of riding her motorcycle as the sun sets and volunteers her time supporting her community. She lives in Ontario, Canada, and can be reached through her website, www.DanielleSaputo.com.

Manufactured by Amazon.ca
Bolton, ON

29855879R00125